THUNDER RUNNER

Poems by Ryan Quinn Flanagan

Kung Fu Treachery Press
Rancho Cucamonga, CA

Copyright © Ryan Quinn Flanagan, 2019
First Edition 1 3 5 7 9 10 8 6 4 2
ISBN: 978-1-950380-21-3
LCCN: 2019937943

Design, edits and layout: John T. Keehan, Jr.
Cover image: Jon Lee Grafton
Title page image: Jon Lee Grafton
Author photo: Shona Flanagan
All rights reserved. No part of this publication may be reproduced or transmitted in any form or by any means, electronic or mechanical, including photocopying, recording or by info retrieval system, without prior written permission from the author.

Grateful acknowledgement is made to the following publications where some of the following poems may have appeared: *Academy of the Heart and Mind, Alien Buddha Press, Anti-Heroin Chic, BlogNostics, Event Horizon, Hanzir, Medusa's Kitchen, Outlaw Poetry Network, Piker Press, Ramingo's Blog, Record – Chicago Record, Scryptic Magazine, Setu, Synchronized Chaos, The Asylum Floor 2, The Beautiful Space, The Fox Poetry Box, The Rye Whiskey Review, Tuck Magazine, Two Drops of Ink*

CONTENTS

I Felt Bad for Swedish Meatballs / 1
A Man Called Space / 2
Those that Grew Up with Stern Fathers Probably Don't Miss the Berlin Wall / 3
Death of a Saleswoman / 7
Plasticine Animals in a Psychological Zoo / 8
Taylor made / 9
Chasing Squirrels Through the Graveyard / 11
Razor / 12
Derek / 13
Sugar Rush / 15
Golems / 16
You're in a State / 17
Imagination / 19
Pinterest / 20
Groucho, by Default / 22
Suffering for my Sins / 23
THUNDER RUNNER / 24
Crags / 25
Sam / 28
Out of Order / 30
Come On Eileen, Your Bath Salts Are Showing / 31
Blue Squirrel Hammock, Dupont St., Little Current / 33
Karl / 34
Fairy Floss / 36
Seeing Other People / 37
Outsourcing my Poems to a Woman with Large Breasts and Small Tweezers / 39
Maypole Dancers / 41

Event Hall / 42

I Am a Firefighter in a Janitor's Body / 45

Sin Bin / 46

Bunker Buster Minds / 48

Deadbeat Don / 49

Action / 51

Olivia / 52

Body Slam / 53

Maybe Alaska / 55

Leaving David / 57

Pink Flamingos / 58

Curry Favour / 60

Last Freedom / 62

One Arm Winston / 63

She kept / 64

CRAZ FUKR / 66

Mole / 68

pawpaw / 70

Jellybean Jars Can Only Take So Much / 71

Crank Calling a Place of Business / 72

PTSD # 7 / 73

Thin People Are Never in the Thick of It / 74

Open for Beeswax / 76

Distillers / 78

Noon, with Lipstick / 79

Qahwah / 81

Do Pigs Sweat? / 82

Liquid Courage Never Tasted So Good / 83

The Leaves Return to Spring Masters / 84

Kickstarter / 85
She Tells Me about a Deer / 87
Hazmat / 88
California Republic / 89
Estate / 92
Sunhat / 93
For V / 95
Double Parked Seagull / 96
Market / 98
Poem for a Child that Has Yet to be Persuaded / 100
Girlfriends / 101
Rattling Flag, Half-Mast / 102
Extremes / 103
Old News / 105
Ringo on Cushions / 106
Coward's Camo / 107
Poking Holes in the Maiden Voyage / 109
Nothing Good Ever Came From Long Island / 111
Caught Slipping / 112
Red Carpet / 113
Blue Air Mail Stickers / 114
Sometimes You Just Know / 115
Go / 117
Vancouver Island Ferry / 118
Colour of the Blues / 119
Wilted Rose / 121
Discarded Blue Surgical Glove / 123
5 Hour Window / 124
Berthing Assistant / 125
The Fur Harvesters / 126

Playing Spin the Bottle with Myself / 128
Six Winston Churchills and a Doorman
    Who Doesn't Care / 129
Canadiana / 131
Time is Not Precious / 132
Duty Free Bigotries / 134
Hank Williams / 135
Red Panda / 137
Love is Just Lust in the Right Lighting / 139
Movie Network / 141
Reserved Parking / 142
Never Tell Them You Are the Words / 144
Conference / 145
Last Chance Laura / 147
Back / 149
Twistin' The Night Away / 150
California Plates / 151
Rat Trap / 153
Business / 155
Steam Punk / 156
Finding the Place / 159
Upon the Death of Peter Cottontail / 160
Happy Songs Sell Records, Sad Songs Sell Beer,
    and Angry Songs Won't Sell at All Until You
    Tweak Them / 161
Customs Agent / 162
Marching Band Parades / 164
FC / 165
Villainy in the Badlands / 166
Dozer / 167

Stem Cell / 168
Heated Conversation / 169
Race Records / 171
Federal Injunction / 172
You get tired / 173
Green Bell Peppers / 175
??? ?? / 176
Jersey City Altar Boy / 177
Texas with Snow / 178
Dirty Socks after Three Days / 180
Fuck Bukowski (2) / 182
PTSD # 95 / 183
The Anarchists / 185
LIVE / 186
Hush Money / 187
Mountain Lion / 189
Double Drive / 191
Hustle / 193
Pitbull live from Miami each New Year / 194
Bracket Buster / 195
Ruins / 196
Last Words / 197
She Bop / 198
Dented Head / 199
Slow Down / 200
Late Fees / 202
Stalker Poem / 203
Tremors / 204
Her phone / 205
Black Stretched Limo / 206

Just Wine / 207
Robocalls / 209
Yellow Placemat / 211
Invaders Must Die / 212
Tag / 213
When You've Watched Too Many Game Shows / 215
Between Handlers / 216
Imagine / 218
God was an Irishman with a Fifty Foot Dick / 220
Whoa Nellie! / 221
Live Bait / 223
Honest Assessment / 224
Thread Count / 225
Leg Work / 227
This is Where They Killed the President / 228
Wantling / 230
The One / 231
Protests / 232
Business (2) / 234
White Feather / 235
Factory Direct / 236
Yule Log / 237
Ask My Dust / 239
Nursing Presentation / 240
Vanticide / 242
To those who call paper parchment / 243
Demolition Expert / 244
Tectonic / 246
An Answer / 247
Renege / 249

Uncivil is the War / 250

Always Cry Wolf / 251

Visible Minority / 252

All Those Stairs / 253

St. Patrick's Day, 2018 / 254

White Devil / 257

Dizzy / 258

Tall Cans / 260

A fight / 261

Staples / 262

28th / 263

Product Placement / 264

Drain Cover / 266

Venture Capital / 268

Breaking Silence, Breaking Wind / 269

The New Minimalism / 270

Bark / 271

Sewer Cake / 273

$3 Dollar Movies / 274

Penny Slots / 275

Shoot Me Before I Shoot You / 276

A Man in Lifts Wants to be Carted Around like a False Ladder / 277

Quick Strike / 279

A Death in the Family / 280

After Lively / 281

Smash Up / 282

Daisy Dukes / 284

It is silly / 286

Crash Dummy / 288

Blow the nose / 289

Sloppy Glow Stick EDM / 291

Compact Car Rentals / 292

Basketball Net / 294

Yo-Yo Man / 297

Flying Pig…Revisited / 298

Good Tidings and All that Stuff / 299

Protagonist Zero / 301

Face Fronds / 305

PTSD # 112 / 306

Grayson / 307

One of Micheline's (for Brenton Booth) / 309

Gloomy Dean / 310

Full Circle / 312

Hallway / 314

No Question of Ownership / 315

And your curious life with me will be told so often that no one will believe you grew old

-Leonard Cohen

I Felt Bad for Swedish Meatballs

The founder of Ikea died last week
and I felt bad for Swedish meatballs.

Knowing everything would change
once Kiss left their makeup.

Once Halloween loses its mystique
it's just creepy people at your door
with kids demanding candy.

The young ones are cute
because they are not yours.

The same way helicopters look nice
patrolling someone else's sky.

But I knew the party was over.
I felt bad for Swedish meatballs.

The way the stores would start closing
like women who no longer
loved you.

Everyone laid off
because the good times
were over.

A Man Called Space

I have been at this too long.
The oils from my fingers have rubbed
off half the letters on the keyboard.
But I still seem to know where they all are.
The fingers keep a steady pace like holding
down a second job. If I were to stop and think
I would lose my spot. It is all reaction.
Muscle memory. I have done this so many times
I just keep doing it without even thinking.
The same way you get so drunk you wake up in
your own bed and don't know how you got home.
You just did. And you will keep doing that because
it has become a part of you now. Still, I wish the letters
had not rubbed off. I liked to sit down to them.
To see them staring back at me and winking.
The numbers are still intact. But I was never big on math.
I miss my letters. Even that bastard Q sounding like K
by other means. I miss my children.
I miss them all.

Those that Grew Up with Stern Fathers Probably Don't Miss the Berlin Wall

my knee slams
against the underside
of the desk

a human metronome

knowing Goethe
would get sick on
rollercoasters

and that the plague
was blamed on rats
just like the downfall
of the mafia

even though I open the windows
this is not a commune

I don't want everyone else's children
running around dirty and naked
so the many orgasms of the East India Company
can find themselves

and the cable bill comes
and I begin to wonder how anyone
can afford all that porn

rubbing skin cells of frustration
off my forehead
for the new human
genome

sleeping on the job
when I can
and working on sleep
the rest of the
time

writing poems that go nowhere
like free market Europe lost
to lipstick roundabouts

and all my big game hunting
has taken place in small musty
bookshops without names

so many piles of books
I can never read

and I flip through a couple pages
of each,
most democratic,

realizing those that grew up with stern fathers
probably don't miss the Berlin wall
at all

and if my fridge must be filled
with something
it may as well be
food

the continuance of the species
is vitally important
to your local cable service
provider

while spelunkers dive deep
into a cave of debt
and guano-faced lovers
lick the insides of your ears
to Dick Clark's New Year's
Rockin' Eve

so that I look at the empty mantle
and think of product placement

how airplanes are human birds
without any of the song

and when I sit in the closet,
it is never for Buddha
my foot against the door
like a church bell wanting
out

on Super Bowl weekend
with all those commercials
that paid millions for a
thirty second spot,

existing in a way the rest of us
never really
do.

Death of a Saleswoman

Of course Arthur Miller couldn't stay with Marilyn. He told her she was the saddest woman he had ever met. Then he wrote it into the script of The Misfits as though she hadn't heard him the first time. What a pickup line, a real panty peeler there: *You are the saddest woman I have ever met.* What woman doesn't want to hear that? And when you hear the playwright speak in such a manner, you really begin to understand Willy Loman. Selling vacuum cleaners on the moon. Or Frank Zappa naming his kid Dweezil and being surprised when things go awry. That final episode of Cheers and the way it was marketed as crackerjack tears. They almost challenged you not to cry, which of course, became a crying contest between attention whores. Which brings me back to old Norma Jean. The blonde bombshell. Happy Birthday Mr. President. And Arthur Miller doing his best Arthur Miller impersonation. This is not to slag off Arthur Miller, only to point out the futility of such an enterprise. Even Joey Di couldn't make it work and he came in Yankee pinstripes. No, I feel bad for Arthur because he could see what others could not. Worse still, he said it. Which is a great thing if you are a playwright but as a lover not so much. And when Marilyn died, the press was relentless. I'm glad he found Inge and started hand crafting furniture. Connecticut is not the best place to die, but it is hardly the worst. A man should be happy if he can be anything. I think Arthur found some of that.

Plasticine Animals in a Psychological Zoo

There are no friendly blades
with such passionate
backing

and the excuses you make
are plasticine animals
in a psychological
zoo

she will not hear them
the walls repainted with
deafness

a fresh coat
to undercut the thriving
mothball market

your excuses are playing

learning how to
hunt.

Taylor made

a mail slot
with an old motorbike
helmet
with a visor you could
throw up and down
and he rounded off
his door
to meet the angle
of the helmet
which he then screwed
into the door
and sanded down the edges
and spray painted
the word: MAIL
in red
over the top
of the helmet
so that his mailman
would understand the
process and appreciate
a different look
and someone called
the city
and complained,
but the by-law officer
quite liked it

if you are to hear
Taylor's telling
of the story
which could be
the truth
or something
else,

but it's a good yarn
regardless
and he still has
the helmet.

Chasing Squirrels
Through the Graveyard

Lay flowers
against the stone
of those that came
before.

The children chasing squirrels
through the graveyard.

Too young to know.

The way they sit down in the grass immediately
each time their angry father
warns them.

Pulling up grass shoots
and throwing them on one another
until their father yells
back at them
once again.

Razor

In the Sudbury madhouse
they made you share
a room
so that you were never alone
and the bathrooms were monitored
for suicides
even though there were
privacy laws against it
and they wouldn't admit it
and you had to approach the nursing station
behind glass
if you wanted a razor
to shave

and the cutters had
to have a monitor
at all times
and return the razor
to the nursing
station

once
hair had been removed
from body

and life had
not.

Derek

worked
for his father
which meant he
was owned and operated
driving that rusted out
animal removal truck
around
with nets and traps
in back
and his wife
took pictures
one of those crime
scene people
that have to go to school
to take their pictures
and when
she went on stress
leave
money was tight
and when she left with
the kids
she said it was not
because he was
in animal removal
even though

he knew it was
and that he was pushing
forty
and still working
for his father
and drinking heavily
in the evenings
as any man will do
when he can't get out
from under the yoke
of his father
just like
all those dead animals
he carried limp
out of the attics of
paying customers
that called about
the smell.

Sugar Rush

the piñata
breaks open
and all your past
lovers fall out

onto the heads
of screaming children
that were expecting
candy

instead of
this.

Golems

golems come out of nowhere
with handfuls of sod
bashing in the skulls of legless dolls
pulled from childhood prams
and that rain you sense is sadness
a torrent for the Chinese New Year
the way you slip on nothing
and fall for even less

I have championed nothing
and never been championed

a true marksman in the
self-inflicted sense

letting you pull at your
many ravages
as though corralling a
willful bucking
rope.

You're in a State

she says
as I stumble down the stairs
and come around the corner
after another day
of writing

but she always says that

so I can't tell if I really am in a state
or if she is just giving me
the business

so I get playful:
what state am I in,
is it Oregon?
I never really liked
all that forest.

Not Oregon,
she laughs.

Is it Vermont?
Doesn't that sound like overly
expensive chocolate?

She laughs.

Please don't let it be Ohio!
The rust belt is just an old chastity belt
that doesn't work anymore.

You realize we are in Canada,
she scoffs.

So how am I in a state?
I think you've been drinking,
I pull her head close to mine.
You should probably go easy on the bottle.
No one likes a lush.

Imagination

is the art of pulling dreams
out of the air
and making them your
own.

Pinterest

We are laying on top of the covers
on a Sunday afternoon
picking through shells for a piece
she wants to build.

Remember this one?,
I ask.

She doesn't
and goes on sorting.

*Why do you always pick the same
little black and white ones,
don't you know this black is oil?*

I grab a large half conch
and hold it to my ear:

YOUR CALL IS VERY IMPORTANT TO US,
PLEASE REMAIN ON THE LINE FOR OUR NEXT
AVAILABLE OFFICER.

She wraps me lightly
on the back of my leg
and smiles.

I think we have enough,
she says.

Then we put all the rest
back into plastic sandwich bags
and wipe the sand off
the bed.

Groucho, by Default

Terry was this
old film buff
that worked
as a spot welder
out in the new
industrial park
and once
on lunch he asked me
which Marx
brother I liked best
and I said Karl
and he said that
Karl was not
a Marx brother
so I said Groucho
because it
was the only one
I knew having never
watched a single
Marx brothers
movie ever.

Suffering for my Sins

I was still a small kid,
but Mrs. Ferron always hated me
because they gave us cotton balls
and this beardless Jesus calendar
and you were supposed to stick one on
each day until his beard was full
at the end of the month,
but I jumped the gun and gave him
a full beard right off
which was deemed sacrilegious
and I was not allowed back at the church
and Mrs. Ferron was so angry with me
that she made me run every bike home
and run back in the dead of summer
to grab the next one and run it back
to her place without a word
and there were six children
which meant there were six bikes
and it was over a mile each way
which meant I had to run over twelve
miles and since I did what I was told
I never rode any of the bikes once
which seemed to make her even angrier
each time I returned to grab another
bike.

THUNDER RUNNER

He worked
at this auto body place
along Bayfield St.
in Barrie
and drove a rebuilt
purple roadster
with black skull decals
and white lettering across
the front windshield that read:
THUNDER RUNNER
and every weekend
he would drag
down gasoline alley
in personalized black
racing gloves
an ex had given
him as a gift
towards a homemade
checkered flag
that used to be a
restaurant table cloth
now waved
by this blonde
who went with
the guy who took bets
and handled the
money.

Crags

I am moving through the streets at night
in a kind of delirious mist.

The houses are darkened.
Cars are parked in driveways
and on the street.

This must be the city that sleeps.
No cars drive by.
No barking dogs.

The yards are fenced off and humble.
I try to whistle but it is all crackers.

When I pass a stone drive,
I stop to kick some stones
along with me.

First in a pile,
which gets gradually smaller
until I only have one left.

I keep kicking it for some distance
until I stop.
I have decided that this is the last rock
on earth and that I am letting it go.

I am letting it become extinct.

It is easy.
I just kick it and then I don't kick it the next time.
And then the rocks are gone.

I open a mailbox and look inside.
There is nothing.
The name on the mailbox says:
The Crags.

And I think of nesting birds.
How the rocks are gone now
so the nests are as well.

I guess it won't be long for the birds.
All those windows without curtains.
And the air is warm and dry.
It could be summer.

But there are no bugs.
It is silent, even my walking.
In my left pant pocket I find a blue
pen cap.

There is no pen just as there will be
no birds.
It is simple.

And I run the pen cap over the ridges
of my fingers.

It is smooth as though they are
no longer there.

I can't remember the last time I ate.
The Donner Party ate, that's for sure.
Sometimes it is good to be alone.
To glide through the clumsy fog of yourself.

Drumlins for arms.
An absence of cholera.
Data harvesters selling off
the ultimate cash crop.

Yes, it is divine to be alone.
Running my nose across my sleeve.
Knowing all the rocks are gone.
And most the birds as well.

Sam

never
liked her name,
said it was a man's
name that parents gave
their daughters
when they wanted a boy,
that it was
a name that made
you a lesbian
by default
and I asked her
if she was a lesbian
and she said
she had to be with
a name like Sam
even though
she wanted a husband
and kids,
but she was adamant
that her parents had
screwed her
and she liked me
because everyone would
call me Brian
even though it wasn't my name

and after a while I just went
with it because
I didn't care
and it was too hard
to correct them
and I remember her
laughing once
and telling me Brian
made me sound
like a bank machine
on the fritz
and how I laughed
because she hated her name
and I didn't care
about mine
and everywhere else
there was a phonebook
of all the others.

Out of Order

One of my favourite paintings of all time
is Bazille's *The Improvised Field Hospital*.
Not because of the craft, but rather the subject.

Imagine the absurdity of going out to the forest
to paint your masterpiece
and you get hit by an errant discus.
How does that even happen?

And you find yourself laid up in bed
while your friend paints you.

The look on Monet's face is priceless.

The only thing that would have made it better
was if Bazille had been cheeky enough
to paint an *Out of Order* sign
with the buckets at the foot
of the bed.

Come On Eileen, Your Bath Salts Are Showing

Come On Eileen
was a huge hit
and Dexys Midnight Runners
ran with it

named after Dexedrine,
I bet the chart people never knew
that,

or the payola people
or the bean counters
and suits

the label people
with money for
fingers

and anyone else who was winning
and stood to lose,

but what an inside joke
for the ages

what a coup

like naming your racehorse
Vanilla Sky
and sending them
to the track
and no one is
the wiser.

Blue Squirrel Hammock, Dupont St., Little Current

I walk down the middle of the road.
Dupont St, Little Current.
Not a single car drives by.

Halfway down the street
I see this blue thing hung in a tree
in the front yard of a home.

It is strung up between two branches.
A blue squirrel hammock right by
the birdfeeder.

And there appears to be a squirrel inside
the hammock.

Swaying back and forth.
It is early afternoon.
I smile.

Karl

thought
he was tough
as everyone does
at that age
and he enjoyed
the bottle
just as his father
and his father before
and relished
the fight even
more
and his mother
always worried that
he would never
come home
and one night
he ran into the wrong one
and although
it is debateable
how tough Karl really was,
having lost
as many walks
as won,
this one pulled
a blade

dug it deep
into the abdomen
then twice
in the neck for good
measure
and Karl bled
out alone
and his mother
started wearing his jacket
around the house
after the funeral
to be closer
to him
while his loyal dog
Chucky laid at the end
of the bed
waiting for ol' Karl
to come home.

Fairy Floss

Follow fairy floss
around the county fairgrounds
long enough
and you begin to see the rollercoaster
in everything

that silly uncomfortable way
vomit sits in your throat
unwilling to pull the trigger

on breaded corn dog weiners
after dark

and darts dull as librarians
challenging you to pop
three balloons
for a prize

on the hustle

while the guess your weight guy
with an ear piece
never misses.

Seeing Other People

He said
she told him
they should see
other people

and I told him that I see
other people everyday
and it isn't pretty

and he agreed,
but said he thought
see was getting back
with her ex

which really isn't seeing
other people at all
as much as it is
revisiting the old ones
to remember why you were
so miserable in the
first place

and I asked him
if he was a rebound,

professional basketball
is full of them,

but he was adamant
that he was not a rebound
and what they had
was real as the moon
in the sky

so I told him to wait it out on the bench
until he was thrown into the starting
lineup again.

Outsourcing My Poems to a Woman
with Large Breasts and Small
Tweezers

*Did you know that you lose about a cup of water an hour
to dehydration when you fly?,*
she asks.

I tell her I did not know that.

*And you lose your taste buds.
That's why the food tastes so awful.
Well, beyond the fact that it is awful.*

I ask her why she is researching all these horrible
things about planes
when we are going to be on one
in less than a week?

*So to sum up:
you become dehydrated
the food is awful
everyone is sick
and sometimes you land?*

*This should give you another poem
to write,* she says.

I think you already wrote it,
I say.

She demands credit.
I tell her I give her more
than that.

But she is adamant,
she wants the
credit.

So you heard it here
first.

Maypole Dancers

It was raining
and out of season
and they found themselves
kneeling inside
chins resting on arms
over the back of the couch
the way bored children do,
staring out at the tall garland-festooned pole
in the field behind their house,
knowing it would be some time before
they could dance again,
with their friends and coloured
strips of ribbon.

Event Hall

I am at this large event hall.

I have a pass around my neck
which you show to the ushers
and they show you
to your seat.

It is obscenely dark.
Loud and disorienting.
I approach the usher and show
her my pass, but when I go to follow
her four ushers converge into one
and then all head off in different
directions.

I can't tell which one I am supposed to follow.
They all look the same.

I pick one and when we get to some seats
a couple with her sits down and she rushes off
before I can get her attention.

I return to the main area and find another usher,
but the same thing happens.

And again.

The last time, I just sit down in an empty seat.
A few minutes later a woman stands over me.
I am in her seat.

I stand up and head back to the main area again.
This time I grab the usher's hand which makes
her most uncomfortable.

I can tell by her grip that she thinks I must be crazy.
Perhaps one of those middle aged men that wear diapers
and have decided to live their life as a baby.

She leads me to this plush horseshoe of couch seating.
It is filled except for one spot at the end.
I sit down.
Everyone else seems surprised by my presence,
so that I think there might be a mistake.
But the usher is gone and it is dark.

The faces at my table start speaking in a language
I do not know and laughing.
I address them in English and they just keep
talking to each other and laughing.

I can tell it is about me.
I don't need to understand the language
to know that.

So I give them the finger.
We all know what that means.

I get up and feel my way back to the main area.
Then down the tunnel back to the parking lot.

It is dark outside and raining lightly.
Now to find my car.

I Am a Firefighter in a Janitor's Body

She jumps up in bed
and seizes my arm with
an uncanny strength.

I THINK I SAW A GHOST!,
she yells,
I SAW, I SAW, I SAW,
I SAW...

She is in a panic.
I pinch the flesh on her wrist.
Bringing her back with pain.

I am almost proud of myself
for thinking so quickly.

I am a firefighter in a janitor's body.
Putting out fires in the bedroom.
The older you get, sleep replaces sex.
I can't explain it.

As soon as I hear her snoring again,
I know I am good for a couple
more hours.

Sin Bin

Who wants to be innocent?
Not me.

I want to be guilty of some things at least.

Not the biggies that get you put away,
but many of the others would be nice.

Don't tell me you are innocent.
Everyone is guilty of something.
Which is fine.

Ignore the sin bin crazies.
They believe Noah and his ark full of animals
were the world's first carpoolers.

Cheated on your diet, guilty.
Jaywalked across a deserted street at four in the morning, guilty.
I did not have sexual relations with that woman,... guilty.
How many little white lies have you told just today?
To keep the peace and some basic working order?

I don't want to be innocent.
Innocence is a lie.

I want to be guilty and alive.
Enjoying the few pleasures we get
for the short time we are here.

Didn't read all of *War and Peace*, guilty.
Toilet papered cars, guilty.
Found $20 on the ground and kept it, guilty.
Impure thoughts…haha, where to start!

Shoplifted food when I was starving, guilty.
Call in sick when I am not sick, guilty.
Give out false numbers at bars, guilty.
Said I loved you when I didn't, guilty…

Bunker Buster Minds

Minds think alike
and then they don't anymore;
not great ones, there is no such thing
and the bunker buster goes astray
so that you are now your neighbour
in a very real way, charred extremities
seared into the rubble, what belongs
to what does not matter anymore:
child, dog, stairwell, cobbler, mother…
all under the large tiresome umbrella
of: Mess.

Those who paid for quiet get their quiet.
Just a flash, then the silence.

Of bunker buster minds.
Of no place at the table.

Deadbeat Don

has kids
with three different
women
and he supports
none of them
hiding his money
putting everything in
his girlfriend's name
and only taking jobs
that pay under
the table
so that his wages
won't be garnisheed
and he can appear
unemployed to
the taxman

and each year
his girlfriend
and him vacation
in Florida,
she has a good job
and knows the
loopholes
so that their drinks

and meals and gas
are write-offs
she gets back
in tax

whoever
said the world
is fair
must have been talking
about someplace
else
'cause this one
is a real humdinger
and Deadbeat Don
takes the cake.

Action

I went over to her house

and —
I said

and nothing,
her father came out with a
curling broom and hit me
all the way down
the street.

So you got some action,
I said.

Yeah, from her father,
what is wrong with you?

There was a lot wrong with me.
Even at that age.
But he didn't need to know
about that.

She told all her friends about it
and he switched schools.

And I kept toilet papering cars
because the Egyptians
had the mummy.

Olivia

for K W Peery

had a thing
for honky tonk
and Reggie
had a thing for Olivia
that went unvoiced
for years
and when Olivia died
last fall
Ernest Tubb did not
go to her funeral
nor Floyd Tillman or Billy Joe Shaver,
Johnny Paycheck, Kitty Wells,
Ray Price, not even
ole Reg,
now married with kids
of his own;
Loretta Lynn's voice
was there
singing:
You Ain't Woman Enough
which seemed a rather
cruel thing to say
at a funeral,
but the song was
Olivia's favourite
even if she was no
longer anyone
else's.

Body Slam

wrestling
with the angels
of others
is never fruitful

they are hardly
even angels

more like
sleep from your eye
that you whisk away
with the back of
your hand

crinkling your way
through bubble wrap boxes
that have come through
the mail

never a pipe bomb inside,
though you'd be fine with that

or some fine powder
like leaving a crematorium
full of pet names

life should be a clumsy celebration
of circumstance
where the living never wrestle
with the dead or their
angels

surrounded by books and moments
and bottles music moments

kisses in the dark
under strange carnivorous
blankets.

Maybe Alaska

You work a meaningless job,
I get it.

Some for the money
and most not even for that.

But you have a job
so you must be going somewhere.

Maybe Alaska.

I was always going nowhere.

Never even had a suitcase
to pretend.

Each night I clocked in
there was no illusion.

The time I lost was mine
and I never got it
back.

And I'd like to say I worked
beside some of the finest men
of my generation,
but I didn't.

You learn survival in the factories.
How to put one night after
the other.

One hour.
One foot.

All those little tricks
to not clock watch,
that is a victory
in itself.

The way your swimming head
walks home in the morning
knowing something has to change
and that you are it.

Leaving David

Turn around
that is my hand
on your shoulder

not some pet shop parrot
chitting back the midnight
particulars

I know why you left David
just as I know why Rhodesia
is not called Rhodesia
anymore

changed your name and number
and started all over
again

how he hit you like a heavy bag
and left you to explain
the bruises,

but I am an old friend,
perhaps your
oldest;

it was good to see you today,
if only from behind.

Pink Flamingos

They
say
things
are
changing

for
the
better

even
though

you
know
they
are
not,

but
hope
is
a
funny
thing,

that
lawn
full
of
whimsical

pink
flamingos

that
wouldn't
burn

anyone
alive.

Curry Favour

She did not have any curry
to cook with
and it was her days off
she was in sweatpants
with the window open
talking to the cats

and she knew I was out
so she asked me to pick up
some curry for her
even though I had never
eaten the stuff before

and when the cashier rang through
the curry powder
I felt the need to tell her
that it wasn't for me

as though I were purchasing a 3-pack
of extra small condoms

and the cashier never even looked up
most professional

which made me admire
this curious little woman
in some strange way
that forces you

to
stare.

Last Freedom

Say something that matters.

Try it.
I have put you on the spot.
Something right to the core.

Even if it is unpopular.
Something you believe.
Just say it.

Surprise me.

You will never feel better.
It is the last freedom.

One Arm Winston

is a pugilist
along the local circuit
and even though he came back
from the war
and left one of his arms behind
they strap both gloves on just the same,
one over his power right
and another taped over his left stump
just below the shoulder
and the stump is just for defense
he holds it high to the chin, pretty good
form actually, *I did a little boxing in the service*
he likes to tell the ring girls between rounds
and he's 3-1 on the circuit so far,
his only loss coming to a southpaw
just out of the slammer
who said Winston really telegraphed
his shots, which is hard not to do
when you only have one hand
to throw and Winston is black
and this guy was white so the rednecks
kept chanting USA! USA!
even though Winston is from Rochester
and served in both Afghanistan
and Iraq.

She kept

trying

but with no
results

imagining
many ancient fertility
gods with stupid
bubble gum names
that were laughing
at her

and each time she failed

it was science
that had failed,

how could they send a man
to the moon,
but not impregnate
a woman?

She asked them
that question
many times.

And the doctors
all looked at each other
saying nothing.

Which didn't help
at all.

CRAZ FUKR

It is in the party favour section
of the Dollar Store
that she feels the need to announce
her great charity to no one:
*I got you puppy, I think I've shelled
out enough!*

I walk by and give her nothing.
The Dollar Store woman in the
sagging green smock doesn't even
turn to look.

She is a veteran of this game.

The kid in the cart is barely two.
He doesn't even talk.
Somehow I know there is
no puppy
and this whole thing
has been for attention.

By the card display
this crazy old bird yells:
*they don't have any funny ones
for funerals!*

Dropping a single blue envelope to the floor
before walking out.

One look at the line
and I leave what I came for
and walk out as well.

Watching this old timer bark back
at a dog in the parked car beside him
as he climbs up into the cab
of a truck with a licence plate
that reads:
CRAZ FUKR.

Sporting an obvious limp.
The sun against my face.

Wondering why most the things
in my pockets are never money.

Mole

You see that mark there on your face?

It's a mole.

*Moles live in the dirt
and feel their way out of blind solitude.
That there is the mark of the devil.*

How can you tell?

*There's a tiny pitchfork in the middle
like a centrepiece from hell.*

I tell him he won't see it if he looks in a mirror.
He's already been seduced.
He's probably already pregnant with
a few of Beelzebub's puppies.

You're an asshole, you know that,
he says,
fingering the mole on his face
like poking at a Jell-O mold.

It has that kind of shake to it.
Like a Persian belly dancer
for new masters.

What should I tell the child services lady?,
he asks.
She wants to know when the power
will be back on.

I tell him I have his back.
The mark of the devil aside.

pawpaw

it is odd
to hear one
speak of simple fruit
as a way of life,
but that is how it is
in these parts:
god, coal, football,
and the pawpaw;
hillbilly mango
Quaker delight…
eaten raw or baked
into desserts,
that custard
down home taste
that brings everything
back
to the kitchen,
deciduous flowering
miracle
of the hills,
so easily bruised
unlike
the hearty people
who call this
land home.

Jellybean Jars Can Only Take So Much

Two old drunks along Shuter Street
try to pick a fight with me.

Ignore them, she says,
let them go.

We are on our way to pick out a cat
from the local humane society.

To give a home to someone
who needs it.

Waiting at the light,
some crazy black dude
fresh off his meds says he's going
to rape my woman.

Keep walking, she says,
he probably has a
knife.

We keep walking
even though I really don't
want to.

Crank Calling a Place of Business

There is much fun to be had
if you are willing to
have it

the scales tip back out
of blue moon
and into your waiting arms

glue
that's known
as paste

bean counters
and jailhouse
confessions

the man
on the other end
of the line

who will not stop
screaming.

PTSD # 7

Those are cluster
bombs in the street
I can't forget the sound
and the screams
and racing down the stairs
and out onto the lawn
I find my childhood
friend Morgan
sitting there in shock
reaching for his legs
that aren't there
anymore
and his dying
body grabs me
by the throat
begs me not to
leave him,
but I can hear
all the other screams
through the fog
and leave him to die
there alone,
the ultimate betrayal,
but I have to find
all the others.

Thin People Are Never in the Thick of It

the wailing wall is the world's biggest crybaby

thin people are never in the thick of it

I count my blessing, a baker's dozen

have you seen the men from the barrio?

the only thing I like about drunkenness
is being drunk

all the rest of this is a trampoline full of hamsters

hype trains are just like real trains,
they come with an engineer

a book in the bag is worth three in the library
(accounting for inflation, someone
has to account)

put the dilly in the dally

send inter-dimensional postcards
written in the 11th person

my passive voice does not make me a Quaker,
the oatmeal people never got the flavours right;
it all fell apart after apple and cinnamon

thick people are rocks that burp

:::::::::: :::::::: :: :::::::::::::::: : ::::::::::::::

that is a lot of colons
for a single prostate exam
to sort out.

Open for Beeswax

Greg
was this guy I knew
from back in high school
with long buck teeth
and straw flat hair that
always looked as though
a farm thresher had
just been run over
his head
and since neither
of us aged gracefully
we could sort of
understand each other
except for his constant need
to troll the bars
well past his prime
looking for younger girls
and the ridiculous way
he would run his fingers
across his chest
and say:
open for beeswax
whenever I asked him
how things were
going

I guess he thought
he was being funny
but some girl's boyfriend
did not agree
and the doctors wired
his jaw shut for a good
five months

and then he went
down south for
work

and this old couple moved
into his place
and took turns dying

so that the house sits
empty now

with a large bay window
in front
where Greg's Siamese cat
used to sit all day

mean mugging
half the known
world.

Distillers

two older men
standing by the mash cooler
waiting to add the cooker malt
while a daughter of one of the two
still learning the business
monitors the still and drawn off
vapours of the cistern room
and later, after adding water
and aging,
these same two men
(every bit as aged as their whiskey)
work their way down a simple clipboard
beside those large oak barrels
ready for the trucks.

Noon, with Lipstick

She wakes up first
puts her arm around
my middle.

I roll over
kiss her on the forehead
like thanking the Blarney
right off of the island.

It is the middle of the day.
The dark noise cancellation windows
have done their job.

And the way she trots off
to the bathroom.
Runs the water and coughs
so I won't hear the ugly
truth of it.

And I imagine her a Chinese spy
even though she is neither slippery
or Chinese.

My arms behind my head
against the headboard,

I listen to the water
from the shower.

Peel the dry pieces off my lips
so we can begin all over
again.

Qahwah

Coffee percolates.
The mind percolates.
The mind must be coffee.
A fresh brew of ideas.
Many percolating for years.

And when the coffee of my ideas
is weak, that is the lean times.

And when it is strong, I am happiest.
Fortified and resilient again.

Only, I am allergic to caffeine.
Which means I am allergic
to my own ideas.

So that I must become more
than myself.

Venture off into all directions
at once.

Leave this body of limits.
For a couple hours at a time.

Do Pigs Sweat?

you hear it often:
sweat like a pig,
but I've never seen it,
pigs must be notorious sweaters
I think to myself
and after breakfast
I look into it
and find that not only
do pigs not sweat,
but that the saying has nothing
to do with pigs at all,
it refers to the way the heating rod
sweats when pig smelting
and the shape of suckling pigs
that results,
so there you have it:
pigs don't sweat
and I eat breakfast
and now I need something
else to fixate on.

Liquid Courage Never Tasted So Good

She jokes
that when I'm drunk
I start speaking properly.

The rest of the time
I stumble over my words
and won't look her in the eye.

I can always tell when you are drunk,
she says,
*you start talking like an English professor
and making sense.*

*And you don't mumble anymore.
Your voice booms with confidence.
It's like a whole other person.*

I tell her to enjoy it while it lasts.
Tomorrow I will be sober.

The Leaves Return to Spring Masters

The leaves return
to Spring
masters.

I'm sure marquee road show Basho
would say much
the same.

All your tears again
like a return to
sadness.

Lock yourself in a hotel bathroom
and only the toilet
wins.

Kickstarter

I climb in the shower and look around.
There is no one with me.

I run my hands over the cold stone tiles.
The grouts lines that lead away from water.

My body will get clean even if my mind will not.
There are numerous soaps that smell
of many things.

It is good to have choices.
Not too many or you become spoiled
and expectant.

More Kickstarters than kick.
Blue skies in the subway.
That lazy sort of mock tenderness.

And there are two towels.
One for the body and one for the head.
I am still young enough to have my hair
so that the second towel does not
get off so easy just yet.

The first towel is a lifer.

It will not be finished until
I am finished.

They will put us both in the ground.
Where the garden spade goes.

But until then I dry off.
Snake my way back into clothes.
Reverse shedding.
Head out to run some errands.

The modern man.
Surrounded by artisanal pizza
and envelopes that lick
themselves.

She Tells Me about a Deer

she drove up on
through the backroads
of Iron Bridge

how large and majestic
he seemed
as she slowed down

to watch him leap over
a large gulley

and gallop off into

the forest
again.

Hazmat

I posted a 7 and a half
minute video
of me in a hazmat suit
peeling carrots
in the driveway

up on social media
and waited for
likes

under the title:
Hazmat

and all I got
was healthcare professionals
throwing shade at me
for trying to be
the sun.

California Republic

We are out in California
for the first time.

On the Huntington Beach pier
watching real actual surfers
command the waves.

I keep waiting for a shark attack,
but it never comes.

Enjoy this, I say,
we will probably never
be here again.

She hugs me
and kisses me on the cheek
so that I know this is important
to her.

She is aware of the geography.

When she buys an overpriced bag
from the kitsch shop
along the pier
that reads:
California Republic

I say nothing.

It is a nice bag.
With the bear and everything.
And this is California.
The Pacific Coast south
and all that gas.

All the way to Mexico,
but no one seems to want to go
that far.

I hear there's a travel warning.
That the cartels are making
things ugly.

Back in our room by the beach
I tell her I am a titan because the gods
got jealous.

Stick a homie in Long Beach
with many comfortable pillows.

She laughs through the dark
and rolls over.

*There's this sandpiper on the beach
that keeps mean mugging me,*
I say.

*If he's there tomorrow
I'm going to say something.*

She is already asleep.
I have always been jealous
of that.

Watching the bathroom light
under the door for the next six hours
and the green light fire alarm
overhead blinking in 28 second
increments.

Until it is time to get up
and walk down to the beach.

That wet thick salt against
your sunglasses
and a sandpiper really asking
for it.

You are human, she says,
*you have to take the high
road.*

I hate that she is
always right.

That squirrely little fucker
with wings really
deserves it.

Estate

He had an estate when he died
that had to be divvied up
according to the will
and I thought: how does one
amass an estate?

I am always running out of everything
so that I have to go back
to the store.

When I die they will have to figure out
what to do with the bag of old batteries
under the bed.

And the lamp in the shape of a moose.
And a few old shirts and pants because they
are the law.

Hardly an estate.
But I will vouch for the shirts.
Some are cotton and breathe
just like fish under
water.

Sunhat

Apparently
some giant pink parachute
landed on the kitchen
table.

That's a sunhat I ordered,
she says,
*to keep from burning when
we are at the pool.*

Could you have gotten it any bigger?
I say.
*The sun won't even know you
are there.*

She says
that's the point,
that I burn as easily as her
so I should know.

I compliment her on her new parachute.
She thanks me.

When we go to bed tonight,
I'm thinking about
wearing it.

I will call it my pink body condom
and roll around in bed
so she doesn't get pregnant.

You can never be too careful.
Especially around scissors.
Blood is falling out of people
all the time.

And all the other fluids.

No wonder my lips are so dry
when I wake up in the
morning.

We can't all have a pink
parachute.

For V

A woman who can
and is willing to express herself
in a whole new way,
there is nothing sexier
than that.

A woman
who is not afraid to be a woman
and never needs her womanhood to be
at the expense of men.

That silly childish way men need to be knocked
as if you can only be defined by the popular slanders
of the day.

Give me a woman who shaves her head
and dresses up in vintage war gear
and tells you the best ways to tease
a prick or pussy with your tongue.

Takes so much flack from other women
and blows it off like an
absent wind.

That is a woman I want to know.
That is a fierce individual spirt
that I am happy to call
a friend.

Double Parked Seagull

I am driving back into town
past the Hillside Walk-in Clinic
when I spot this overstuffed seagull
sitting in an otherwise vacant
parking lot.

He is double parked.
Spilling over the yellow line.
Taking up two spaces with
his sheer size.

His eyes are a devilish red.
Staring straight ahead.
Never once deviating.

I search where he is looking.
There is nothing.
This bird is a stoic, I think
to myself.

He has one hell of a
poker face.

When I pull into my drive
the front light is still on
from the night before.

I welcome the sun
on my arms
for some minutes
before walking
in.

Market

The market was the best.
We could walk between the hustles
and imagine the consequences.

And the subway down into the city
cost next to nothing
back then.

All those people between the kiosks
and the bookstore I always went to after.

That large yellow banner of discount everything.

Not knowing what writing was,
but still searching it out
on weekends.

And the way we went to eat afterwards.
And how she ordered a salad
when she wanted a burger
because we were still
dating.

And that long wet kiss
on the platform
before my train back east
to Warden
and her train west
to Kipling.

Back out of the city.
The morning after.

Trying to explain the many marks
on her neck
to her grandparents
who understood just fine,
but wanted to give her
the business.

Poem for a Child that Has Yet to be Persuaded

A child
can still dream.

Adulthood
is the lost war
for that dream.

A capitulation.

A blind acceptance
that what has come before
is good enough
and what could have
been

too painful to ever
remember.

Girlfriends

He had a girlfriend.
Which was more than any of us
could say.

But they hounded him mercilessly
until he broke up
with her.

Even though
she was one of the only ones
at our school having
sex.

And when the first of us
got a girlfriend,
he lead the chorus
of jeers.

But no one seemed to care anymore.
They were all busy getting
girlfriends.

Rattling Flag, Half-Mast

Today is not a good day to die.
I have decided.
Sitting on a chipped red park bench
listening to the birds sing.

There is a slight wind off the water.
And a flagpole beside me.
The flag is at half-mast.
Rattling against the pole.

Someone must have died.
It could be for that hockey team
that crashed their bus.
I cannot be certain.

And the birds keep singing.
They seem most pleased with themselves.
I fill my lungs with air and exhale.

Today is a good day.
I have decided.

Extremes

I should
have known
there was a problem
when my cousins
dared me
to eat everything
at that buffet
and I got sick
trying

not just once,
but even after they
were gone,

returning to the same
all-u-can-eat buffet
many times over
twenty years

trying my best
to make the kitchen
run out of
food

before
I ran out of
myself

which
at that time
I believed could
never happen.

Old News

He can't seem to get out of his own way.
Like he's the type of guy who can walk into
an empty grocery store and complain
that he can't reach the cash because the
lines are too long.

And nothing ever happens for him,
so that he is never happening.

When I sit down to an old newspaper
dated three days ago
left by another patron,
I think of him.

But never too long.
The world is a busy place.
And when my order is up,
his time is as well.

Ringo on Cushions

She is in the basement sanding down wood
shelving and applying a second coat
of paint.

I hear her working away
like a blacksmith with
benefits.

As I sit on the couch
and imagine myself the Ringo
of couch cushions.

Drunk on wine
and trying to keep up
with the others.

Laughing at everyone's jokes
because I can't think of any of
my own.

Sprawled out over George, Paul,
and John.

Knowing the buttons on my shirt
can't last forever.

Coward's Camo

Planes never fall out of the sky
onto waiting hunters
in coward's camo,
you never hear of it,

I always imagined such things
would be reported
in the popular
press,

the press
just being all the popular kids
from high school
with hair and
make up

all over again

in a world
that never farts
or drinks too
much

where unicorns
run all the networks

and tax havens
provide billionaire
hide and seekers
with all the best places
to hide.

Poking Holes in the Maiden Voyage

I love sinking the ship
poking holes in the maiden voyage,
everything I do predicated
upon this simple notion
of upset.

The Love Boat
stood up at the
altar.

A fork in the road
instead of a
spoon.

I am the joker,
the fool.

Only serious enough to
gain employment.

Hell, just last night
I posted a message up
to social media
that read:

Just watched Dunkirk.

*Was quite upset when I realized
it was not about Captain Kirk
and his various space
dalliances!*

If you are wincing right now,
realize you are not alone.

I have seen that face nearly four times
as much as my own.

I will have to check with accounting,
but I think my numbers
are accurate.

Nothing Good Ever Came From Long Island

Don't say nothing good ever came from Long Island.
Lou Reed came from Long Island,
although he became New York.
Along with Andy Warhol, Frank O'Hara, Hubert Selby Jr.,
and the New York Dolls.
And Times Square before they cleaned it up.
Ginsberg, Burroughs and the boys celebrating the bomb
instead of the peace.

That is my New York.
You can have the rest of it.
Especially the Empire State building.
That thing is tall as tales
and doesn't even play
basketball.

Caught Slipping

Down at the ice rink
by city hall
a young woman in white skates
has her legs give out from under her
so that the young man she is with
has to react fast to catch her
which he does forming a basket
out of his arms
and the woman laughs and steadies
herself by grabbing hold of the
young man's shoulder
before they are off again
holding hands on the far side
of a busy rink.

Red Carpet

Who are you wearing?

What I am wearing is a shirt.
Who I am wearing is a question
you would ask Ed Gein.

Blue Air Mail Stickers

We are thinking of going to Australia
for what the professionals call
a work holiday.

She will nurse
and I will hustle.

And the woman we mail packages off with
at the Rexall tells us that she had the chance
to go to Australia many years ago,
but that she chose England.

And there is nothing to say to that.
Not even the weather.

So we just smile
and wait for her to weigh the package
and put on the blue air mail
stickers.

That arrive
on the other side
of the world.

Like grammatically correct
distress signals.

Sometimes You Just Know

Two to a table
that is how you sit
hands in the lap
across from one
another

most proper
by the window

ignoring the numerous drunks
that knock on the
glass

with many unsavory gestures

leaving the wet
of their tongues
behind

and she tells me
about how she never drinks
because both her grandparents
are drunks,
that they can't stand each other,
but that marriage is
for life

and I tell her my basement apartment floods
each Spring
like the Titanic taking
on water

and she laughs in that silly awkward way
that snakeskin wallets
are funny

and not having to ask for her hand
we walk down by the harbour

sharing lives
that could have been
bestsellers if anyone
had been

listening.

Go

misguided
as it may seem
to start the
fire

there
was never
anything

beyond the
flame.

Vancouver Island Ferry

It is still dark out.
We have made our getaway.
In the middle of the night.
With all our worldly possessions
in tow.

A couple bags.
Rather pathetic.
And we are standing on the deck
under an incredible wind.
The waves slamming up against the hull
and splashing over onto us.

She says she thinks she's going to be sick
and heads back inside.

I watch the blinking lights disappear
in the distance.

Before being thrown back across the deck.
I get up and head inside.

She is sleeping on our belongings
and I decide to join her.

Colour of the Blues

You wanted to be on The George Jones Show
if you were starting out.
Johnny Cash was a regular so he could
make his break.

Merle Haggard too.
Tammy Wynette.

I only think of this now because
of lost sobriety.

Ears big as turnstiles
that make loudspeakers out of all
the crisp dark whispers.

I find I return to things
these days.

Old records, locks of hair
hatcheted off into the waiting
basket of good grooming.

Not for reasons of nostalgia
so much as survival.

And blood,
do not forget
the blood.

The mess we make of ourselves
is sometimes the only hope
of others.

Wilted Rose

knew she was getting older
and that her charms
were now the charms
of others,

that both her sons were
in prison
because of meth

and that she had
meth tongue
because her teeth were gone,
that simple dry mouth
way
she would flick out
her tongue
like a salamander
and sit in chairs that had
always been
there

burning garbage
in the front
yard

and talking about
the cousins that had
once raped her

and how god was good
if you didn't think about any
of the rest of it.

Discarded Blue Surgical Glove

I am walking across from the hospital
along Meredith St.
in Little Current.

Just down from the Hawberry Motel
across from the Shell gas station.

I look down into the culvert
by the road
and see a discarded blue
surgical glove.

It is flipped partially inside out.
Stained with a strange yellowish colour.

Two nurses walk down from the hospital
and head in the opposite direction.
They are in their scrubs.

It must be shift change.
Someone is missing a glove.

5 Hour Window

I cannot imagine my windows
only being there for
5 hours.

What happens then?
An open air intrusion of bugs
and bird?

Open concept to
the masses?

But that is the present
humanitarian reality.

I can't imagine
what I would do without
my windows.

A few of them
frosted over
for effect.

Berthing Assistant

It is dark by the time we arrive.
Sitting in a plane on the tarmac
at Pearson International.
The pilot announcing over the PA
that we have arrived early
and that there is no grounds crew
present to help berth the plane.
He has notified the tower
and we are just waiting.
I am in the window seat back
because the wife had it on the way down.
Most democratic of us, I know.
It takes about twenty minutes for a vehicle
to speed up and for some kid with glowing
orange wands to direct the plane.
By the time we get off, we have to rush
to the other side of the airport.
We have a connector flight up north
to make.

A forty-five minute jumper
into the dark Canadian
wilderness.

The Fur Harvesters

It is easy to run off in fifty different directions.
This body here is not so much a liability
as it is a starting point.

An entry level position in the cosmic gusto.
Rambunctious daycare children with tripwires
for lungs.

There is never a decent fall guy when you need one.
I search the yellow pages for Dial-A-Patsy
and come up empty.

What I like about the winter is that it is quiet.
Everything is dead or hibernating,
I don't care which.

And the way my knuckles crack
like opening a fresh beverage.

There is a fluency there
that escapes the common
door-stop.

I am gaining weight, I can feel it.
Not so much physically, but in other ways.

The eyes droop with prune juice regularity.

Past lives keep calling at inopportune times.

If I were a taxidermist,
I would stuff the shrapnel bomb of my head
full of ideas and rusty nails.

The fur harvesters meet on the first Wednesday
of each month.
I saw their ad in the paper.

Right beside the Men of Song.
For a good time, just
call Phil.

To be clear, I did not call Phil.
Advertising does not work on me
the same way Friday does not work
for you.

There are hurdles to be overcome
and hurdlers to overcome
them.

One always falls after training for 4 years.
Hell, I do that almost every second day.
No assembly required.

And now you have the goods
and many of the bads
as well.

Playing Spin the Bottle with Myself

I take out my gum and pucker up
because rules are rules.

I do not run the show.
The bottle does.

Where it ends up is anyone's guess.
I am nervous and sweating.
It has landed on me again.

Peer pressure demands I should slip
some tongue.

Now I am really sweating.
On the floor by the bed.

Another bottle beside me
to lower inhibitions.

What a horrible sweaty
game!

Six Winston Churchills
and a Doorman Who Doesn't
Care

It was all coming together.
One of us had a car he had leased
from his uncle soon after his
sixteenth birthday.

And this cigar shop opened up
that sold to minors.

And our horrible fake IDs
which would only work at this one club
downtown so that we dressed
in our father's shirts and grew out
our few wisps of facial hair,
letting the most facial of us
go first so they would ignore
all the others.

And I'm guessing they just didn't care.
How could you?

Six idiots inside
all smoking cigars
and choking.

Six Winston Churchills
in Hawaiian shirts four sizes
too big.

Daring each other to approach the bar.
The woman with silver chain mail
over her breasts that came by
with a tray of empties
every so often.

Canadiana

is a funny thing

not at all
like Americana

which knows what
it is

and confidently champions
the cracking of the bell
bride to banner,

Canadiana
simply knows it is
not Americana

and defines itself
solely by that

(by what it
is not)

without ever knowing

or even wanting to know
what that could

actually
mean.

Time is Not Precious

If Time is so precious
why do we all want to sleep
ten hours a day?

Or sit on the toilet
for 45 minutes
flipping through magazines?

Seems to me
that Time isn't precious
at all.

The West coast
flies to the East coast
and loses three hours without
a care in the least.

Ever seen those people pile off the plane?
Happier than a stag party ready to get shitfaced.

I haven't worn a watch
since 1996.

That should tell you something.

And if it doesn't, not to worry.
There are many others that want to tell you
everything about themselves.

I need my sleep
so I have to be going
now.

Enjoy the massacre.
And always with a smile.

Duty Free Bigotries

A single scratch on your face,
you must be a fighter.

No one questions the long nails
lost to sleep.

Sitting in airports by the baggage carousel
waiting for your underpants to arrive.

Running your feet over cold tiled floors.
Nodding off into spotted hijinks.

With your Sammy Davis shoulders
and many duty free bigotries.

Fluttering hummingbird eyelids
hunched over and dry in the mouth.

This could be a terrorist attack.
Women free before eleven.

Your name floating around cyber space
like a sweaty lily pad.

Hank Williams

had
spina
bifida

eleven
number
one
hits

and
many
pills
and
bottles

and
on
New
Year's
Day
at
the
age
of
29

out
front
an
all
night
diner

someone
asked
if
he
wanted
to
eat

last
words:

I
do
not.

Red Panda

I remember
that we had to go to the Toronto Zoo
to see the red panda

because it was not like
all the other pandas
we had seen
before

and how my father balked
at the price of parking
as though the northern lights
should be in the trunk

but we had to see the red panda
that had been on the news

so that my father bit the bullet
and paid the price

and when we got there
all you saw was trees and woodchips
in the enclosure

and I remember looking back at my father,

how they told us the red panda
was rare and rather shy
so that we stared at a couple of trees
with nothing in them

before moving on
to the reptile enclosure
where anything that spits poison
has to be half-
dangerous.

Love is Just Lust in the Right Lighting

You have nothing to lose.
I am less than nothing.

That cigarette
smoked to the filter
in the gutter
that you walk over,
that is me.

Where I am coming from
if there is a place
to come from.

On your way to cigarette breath
and unrequited love
which is just lust
in the right lighting.

No need to cut all the trees
out of the forest.

We have the money line:
Love is Just Lust in the Right Lighting

Everything beyond that is gravy.

The body in bed beside you is warm
and truculent and half literate.

When you laugh, it is a shared laugh.
When you spit into the sink,
there is nothing there.

Movie Network

She has ordered the movie network
to her monthly bill

and I ask her what movies she wants to see

and she says she doesn't know,
but she wants to see what she's been
missing.

What if you've been missing nothing?
I ask.

Then we're paying for nothing,
she answers.

That's what I'm afraid of,
I say.

As she waves me off
just like she always
does.

And I think of smog.
How it just sits there
like sweaty track pants
in an internet café.

Heavy over everything
so that I suddenly find it
hard to breathe.

Reserved Parking

I am sitting in the car
in reserved parking
in the Soo
with the keys while the wife
is in her job interview
so that we don't get towed
and I watch these two kids
who think they are being discreet
make a drug transaction.
The first turning off down an alley
and the other heading back
to the discount motel with
the cardboard covered windows.
It is too early for all of this.
I close my eyes and rest my head
against the window.
Opening them every so often
to see the sign posted in front
of me that reads:
Reserved Parking
NECCAC
North East Community
Care Access Centre
--
CLIENTS.

And people come and go.
Lots of raggedy women and young girls
with their mothers.
I think it might be an abortion place,
but I can't be sure.

Then the wife comes back
and we head over to the Station Mall
to do a quick shopping.

Less than a mile from the
US border.

Never Tell Them You Are the Words

He says he is homeless
and passes the bottle
and you are smart enough
to not say that you
are a poet

to point out
that your woman believes in you
in a way her creditors
do not

and that you still have all your teeth
even though they are
rotting

and the way he coughs into his gloved hand
with the fingers cut away for dexterity
and shows you the blood
so you know such things are tubercular

and not wanting to be another one
of deathbed Edgar's tell-tale hearts,
I move away,

to a brand new city
when I can.

Conference

It's funny how the world has changed
in just a few years.

Her hairdresser called me a kept man
and she didn't correct her.

And flying down to the city,
she has gone off to her conference.

Something about keeping records
that bring a lot of money
into the hospital.

And I yawn and scratch myself,
knowing I am supposed to meet her
at 4pm.

It is just after noon.
I have slept eleven full
hours.

After I shower,
I will visit the markets.

A few bookshops
down in the fashion
district.

She has left $20 on the desk
by the door
in case I see something
I like.

Last Chance Laura

was always
about to become a nun
or an artist
no one could be sure
which
and she was a looker
in that wholesome
small town way people
look at bread
and at parties all the boys
would tell each other
that last chance
Laura was going to be
a nun
so if you wanted
the action
it was now
or never
and for her part,
she loved the attention
if not the nickname,
kept the game going
all through high
school,
last I heard
she went onto college,

one of
the smart ones
and even though
her breath always smelled
of peach schnapps
and I doubt
she ever wanted
to become a nun,
I have to admit
the school of theology
would be lucky
to have her.

Back

He wants to know right away.
Will I be back?
I tell him I will even though I won't.
He seems satisfied with that.
I have given him something to hold onto.
A lifeline.
But I won't be back.
It is a long walk to get there.
Twice that distance if I come back.
But everyone needs to know.

Even if what they know is a lie.

I wonder how my back looks as I walk away.
Probably hunched.
A little wrinkled in this shirt that won't
fit right.

The ground being the ground.
The sky being the sky.

No surprises.

Twistin' The Night Away

I am not having children
the same way I am having
orgasms.

This is an economic decision.
From the central bank.
A question of personal enjoyment
as well.

We are selfish.
No crime against that.
This life is ours to live
and we intend
to live it.

For no one else
as long as we can,
reverse cowgirl
to old Sam Cooke
records

that almost fuck
themselves.

California Plates

Parking
in
the
underground
with
California
plates

looking
to
win
big

in
the
cemetery

of
desert
lights

where
Bugsy

bet
it
all

and
lost

big.

Rat Trap

People who set rat traps
in the basement
out of fear
but shop in
underground malls
confound me.

This is not a first year philosophy paper.
This is not Descartes spinning in circles
over the knob of a bat
and stumbling around the square dizziness
of himself to rapturous applause.

Do you think that shirt is so much cheaper
by the subway?

That no one can see you
shopping like a miner
for gold?

And it's always so clean down here.
My shoes slip across the marble.

With no money to spend,
I sit and watch all the others.

On a bench
by the popcorn vendor.

Kicking my shoes off
like someone fresh out
of the job.

Business

I remember walking through the heart of the business district
downtown as a teen and throwing up my arms thinking
is this all they got?
I've seen a dog park full of more business
and everyone was in a black suit so that you couldn't tell
one from the other, it looked just like a funeral except
for the briefcases and everyone on phones in a hurry.
I guess I could of read the situation wrong, I was young
and kept to my own and didn't involve myself in anyone's
business, so business could have been bust or booming,
I couldn't tell. But I knew enough even back then to know
that if anything could go one way or the other, it would
probably go both ways before too long and neither
was the way I wanted to go.

Steam Punk

We are at the Lowe's in Sudbury
looking at plumbing fixtures.

Or put more correctly,
she is looking and I am standing
with my arms crossed at the end
of the aisle

waiting for the end
of the world.

This is what I want,
she says,
but it's not the right size.

How would this look if I spray painted it black?,
she asks.

*I don't care if you paint my ass green
and call it a leprechaun,*
I say.

Why don't you look around the store,
she says.

So I look around the store.
It is full of stupid people buying
stupid things.

When I return to plumbing,
she is still at it.

Only now she has a cart.
Which means more money.

Our new bathroom is going to look great!

As long as it isn't steam punk,
I say.

Think of it as industrial.

Instead of arguing,
I turn and walk off to look
around the store again.

Sitting in the patio furniture section
for awhile
imagining a cooler full of beer
at my feet
under the zipper tight mosquito net
on sale.

And standing over the many buttons
on the stainless steel barbecues
knowing half the nobs are merely
decorative, but will sell for sticker price
because of the season.

The pallet of charcoal right there
like a best friend swooping in
after a breakup.

And when I return, she is finally done.
$82 later we have many silver things
that will soon be black things.

Just trust me,
she says.

So what can I do?

One thing
becomes something else
until I am no more.

And she wants to hear that she was right.

That you love it
almost as much as
her tongue
piercing.

Even though bathroom fixtures
have never meant that much
to any man.

Finding the Place

He said it was an old biker bar
from after the war
and we walked up on this field
of discarded tall cans
and joined a circle of people
that reeked of straight
bloodlust.

Looks like we found the place,
I said.

He nudged me in the side
with a strange excitement.

Two combatants in the middle
ripping each other apart
to a wall of jeers.

Torn down
like that old biker bar
from after the war
that we had talked about
on the long bus ride
West.

To where the sun
sets on everything
but itself.

Upon the Death of Peter Cottontail

Run
rabbit
run

girlfriend's
got
a
gun

page
turn
the
page

this
book
is

almost
done.

Happy Songs Sell Records, Sad Songs Sell Beer, and Angry Songs Won't Sell at All Until You Tweak Them

Bowie was a chameleon.
Sure he had to chew his way out of his
first tail, but that is how it is with management.

Your first contract.

You go one way
and the money goes
the other.

And things were really draconian back then,
you think it's bad now.

When John Lennon helped him write Fame
at Electric Lady Land
it was a nasty
song.

You can still hear Lennon chanting *aim*
in the backing vocals.

This is Bowie pulling the trigger,
but not quite
because he switched it
to Fame.

Customs Agent

Do you have anything to declare?

No,
I sighed.

Are you sure?

Yeah,
I sighed.

The customs agent looked at my wife who smiled.

Afterwards, my wife said she was proud that I did not say anything weird.

You probably shouldn't have sighed,
that almost got us another trip
to the Welcome Center.

But –

I know you think your jokes are funny,
she said,
but other people do not.

At least you like my jokes.

She laughed.

See, I can always make you laugh.

She rolled her eyes
and took my passport
back.

We still had a long drive
ahead of us.

Marching Band Parades

rain made my day
marching band parades

child on shoulder points
tossed baton accolades

stores open late
clouds in the harbour

courthouse colonnades
waving shopkeeper

bedtime story rain
child under blanket
sleeps

boats in the harbour sway
marching band parades.

FC

stands for football
club

it also means Freedom Club
according to the Unabomber
who etched the initials into each
of his bombs

and yes,
he had an affinity for the
colour green,

but so does the estate of
Henri Toulouse-Lautrec
and Greenpeace

so I wouldn't disgrace
an entire colour

and standing at the pumps
the petrol station is playing Smash Mouth
doing a very peppy version of the Monkees I'm a Believer
over the loudspeaker

which makes me feel bad about being there,

but I cannot help it
because I am nearly out
of gas.

Villainy in the Badlands

Villainy in the Badlands
again, seems a little redundant
to me

like forging a few billion John Hancocks
out of their only snake venom
and wearing your epiphanies around
like boots

and the fangs of the spider
and the glyphs of ancient rock

dance routine deliriums
parched of their water

even the abandoned filling stations
by the highway skeletonized

in a careless dusty death
four out of five morticians
can't help but recommend.

Dozer

He is one of those grotesques.
Not quite Victor Hugo going full on hunchback,
but getting there.

A dozer.
On the subway out of the city.
Like those big head caricatures
that get everything right
but proportion.

Nodding off
in abrupt nasally snores
that keep choking
awake.

Falling against his fellow passengers
that shoulder him away.

In full uniform.
Drooling down the side
of his face.

Standing room only.
And hardly even
that.

Stem Cell

research
is always being protested
and funded
and protested again
so that after
awhile
it becomes hard
to figure out
where the funding
begins
and the protest
stops

in much
the same way
you dig a hole
into the wet
crimson earth

and wonder
about all the rain
in the sky.

Heated Conversation

He found an old cassette he had made in his youth
of his mother yelling at him to get out of bed for school
and him yelling back that it was a snow day
even though it was May

and the tape went on like that
mother and son back and forth for
over three minutes

and to celebrate his estranged
mother's birthday

he preheated his oven
and threw the tape in it
for twenty minutes
at 350

so that when he opened the oven

only a tiny black blotch
remained.

Then he put socks over his hands
and checked the mail.

A bill from the phone company
and one from the city.

And cutting eye holes in a sheet of tinfoil,
he thought of James Dean changing a tire
at the Griffith Observatory.

And trips through a jungle
so thick it swallowed the best
of you.

Race Records

Don't think for a minute,
that is all –

okay, I'm back after someone's
lost weekend intermission

listening to race records
because that is what they used
to call them

all the good ones you can't put down

that speak to you
and that little person inside
who runs the show

no minstrels for me, thanks

my vitals come in an old blue
milk crate

scratched to hell
like nobody's Diablo

an archeologist's dust
over everything.

Federal Injunction

There was a federal injunction
from the court
and since no one knew what that meant
they continued racing shopping carts
down the hill,
one curled up inside the cart
and one pushing,
two teams and a girlfriend
with a camera phone
to catch the action.

You get tired

of apologizing to her
in the morning
for punching her in your
sleep

in a panic
fighting for your
life

things so terrible
that you tell
no one

sometimes
the results are more serious
than others

and just when I think I could not
feel any worse,
she tells me that when she rolls over
she has taken to throwing
her hand up just
in case

which
makes me feel

like a total piece of shit
even though there is no way
to stop it

in spite of the many
medications.

Green Bell Peppers

I wish I was not allergic to green
bell peppers
the way the spray foam insulation
on all those home improvement shows
seems impervious to everything.

As though the gods in the walls
have your back but never
brag it.

As I watch six straight hours
of long haired cats
being combed out with
sponsorship.

And realize
the world is every bit
as ludicrous as I always
felt it was.

??? ??

I like poems that ask questions.
Not so many as to become an interrogation,
but enough to show a willful curiosity
and strident unknowing.

Poems that pretend to have all the answers
are lies just as people that pretend to have
all the answers.

One writes the other
and they may as well be
the same.

I like to be surprised.
A decent poem likes to be surprised
too, I should think.

I don't know,
but I think.

Jersey City Altar Boy

A young Richard Kuklinski would
glue two cats together and watch them
maul each other to death
in a panic

and when asked about it
by a prison shrink years later
he lamented that you couldn't stick around long
because it made quite a racket

and then he smiled as though
he had just told a dirty joke
at a party

looking for that fear in the eyes
of others
that so turned him on

even though he wouldn't
admit it.

Texas with Snow

I was
talking with this yank
who called these parts
Texas with snow
and he wasn't wrong,
nothing
but hunters and fishermen
up in these parts
driving
two ATVs in opposite
directions to skin
their deer
baiting bears and
building huts
for ice fishing,
a church on every
corner
and gun racks
mounted on every
truck
and somehow
I like the place,
it is quiet
and simple here,
cut right out

of the beautiful
Canadian wilderness
which is
more than I can say
for a lot of other places
which is
why we bought
a house
and settled
down.

Dirty Socks after Three Days

A man is just a woman with a different sense
that smells of fried food after three days of work
and you get to wanting the woman again
because your nose runs the show
and the woman is there for you
without holes in her underpants
which is nice

as much as she can be here
or change you
like dirty socks after
three days,

really
it is all about the
socks

and the smell

so that the men
and the women don't
really matter
at all

and the pillows
with the dried bloodstains
on them

almost fluff themselves

into hours of restless
sleep.

Fuck Bukowski (2)

the dead
do not have
a voice

so that even the daughters
of mothers

that never shared a bed

with uncle Buk
claim orgasm by
proxy

which seems as meaningless
to me as non-alcoholic
beer.

PTSD # 95

I come home
and my whole family
is dead,
my father sitting upright
in bed
with an axe through
the top of his head
like a whole new haircut
and my mother is in the kitchen
parts of her have been cut away
from the whole and left to steam
in the toaster,
the fire alarm is going off
and that reek of human flesh
that never leaves you
and the head of my brother
is in the basement
where the VCR goes,
his body in the shower
getting clean
and I can't find my sister
in that house along
Tower Drive
that flooded each spring,
an infestation of ants
through the walls

carrying part of my family
away and I hear myself scream,
I actually hear it –
and then I am awake
and sweaty and being consoled
by my wife
for something I can never explain
using simple ordinary words,
she doesn't even want to know
and I thank her
for that.

The Anarchists

ran through the streets
in ski masks

smashing in the windows
of big name eateries

and hurling Molotov cocktails
at all the banking conglomerates

in groups of seven
to ten

with access to the underground

so the authorities
could never nab just
one of them.

LIVE

I
don't
know
how

to
put
it

any
other
way

so

I
won't.

Hush Money

We are sitting in a room full of computers.
At her college so she can have a better living.
And the way I swivel around bored in my chair beside her.
Writing obscenities on the blackboard to meet
the morning coffee crowd.

They have cameras, she says,
I have to graduate.

Tell them I am some insufferable flirt
that followed you in
and that you never saw
me before.

*They will probably give you a few dollars
hush money just to keep things quiet
in the current climate.*

She laughs
and asks me to just sit still
and let her print her
assignment off.

Then we drive home
in a rental car because she is
just learning to drive.

With right of way
in a red two door
hatchback.

Almost running over some school kids
on the green
with half a dozen knapsacks
full of homework

they will never
finish.

Mountain Lion

I've seen the pictures.
Mountain lions come to rest
on the welcome mat
by the front door.

Calling in sick
because an apex predator
is sleeping it off on your
front stoop.

That is what you get for living five minutes
from the wild.

You are not a vegetarian
and neither is anyone
else.

Sometimes the wild comes
to you.

And you are smart to stay inside.

Some cats are too big
for the litter box.

When I stand in front of mirrors
my hair seems to be going off
in all directions.

Like a confused roundabout.

And the authorities you called
will try to scare the damn thing away
before they shoot it.

My hair running off
in all directions.

Double Drive

He offers to get me laid
because my parents have allowed
him to come over and work on his car
in our double drive.

On that corner lot along Meadowland Avenue.

He is a few years older than me.
From Nicaragua.
Set back a few grades because
of the education system.

Which means he came to girls
faster than us.

And his girlfriend has a girlfriend
that will do anybody.

Except I don't just want to be anybody.
Plus, I don't know my way around a girl
any more than I do his car that won't start
and leaks oil.

And it's supposed to be a camping weekend.
Suppose she wants me for the entire weekend.
I don't even know what to do once.

So I play things cool.
Pretend I am keeping my options open.
Even though we both know I have no options.

And it is a horrible feeling.
To not be that all dominant red-blooded male
of the world.

To speak in tongues in my sleep.
Which is also not good if you are camping.

I did like his sister though.
I had no problem talking to her even though
she was many years older.

Maybe I liked that it was easy.
I have always been a staunch proponent
of minimal effort.

Which reminds me,
don't ever tell the
girls that.

They seem to be big on effort
in a way I never have been.

Hustle

The phone rings. Is this the hustle then?
It doesn't feel like a hustle. Maybe it is just
a good one and that is why it doesn't feel
like a hustle. And it is hard to not be part of
something. People keep saying you are
a part of it until you can't remember if you
are or aren't. And it doesn't matter anyways.
Enough people believe it and that will never
change for them. And it is not a good feeling.
If this is the hustle. If this is all there is.
The phone stops ringing. My ears are not
so lucky. Never a moment of peace.
Back to the hustle, I suppose.

Pitbull live from Miami each New Year

She wants to watch Pitbull live from Miami each New Year. Tells me it is amazing that nobody ever sweats even though we have been there and know the heat. That is where we learned about finger sweat. Our thick Canadian blood was no match. We even rented a red sports car with a retractable roof to look cool. We still looked hot. Those red British descent faces you see right before a stroke. And I guess we got some sun. The man working the x-ray at customs joked that he would hazard a guess that we spent some time at the beach. And the itch doesn't really get to you until you arrive home. And just when you feel back in your own skin again, she wants to watch Pitbull live from Miami. And it all comes rushing back again. How that large thing that bounced off your leg in open waters could have been a fish and not a shark, but who can say? It felt big and purposeful, that is all I know. And the jellyfish were everywhere. Like walking through downtown New York at rush hour with bare feet. And four minutes after midnight I go to bed. It will be winter here for another five months. All those imbeciles smooching in the New Year. Under heavy security, so the candles never become the cake.

Bracket Buster

When
you
can't
control
the
variables

you
are

pissing
in
the

wind.

Ruins

I guess ruins have to be ancient
for people to want to go stand in them.
Pay admittance and fly whole continents
to do so.

When a fire or some other horrible disaster happens here,
nobody pays to stand inside the ruins.

They deem it unsafe
and knock the damn
thing down.

And argue with the insurance companies
that never pay and always have an out.

And no one calls them ruins.
Even though that is what they are.
They call it a tragedy.
Hardly ever stopping to smile
for selfies.

Last Words

If there
is anything
left to
say

I hope you
say it

and that

the nodes
left behind for
ears

are listening

and that
the stripper
of your cake
makes all

the
difference.

She Bop

We walk into the new bank
that has just opened up
in the lower plaza.

No one has money.
We are first in line.

The girls seem surprised.
My wife is just here to make sure
her changed password
has been recorded
after the latest hack.

While Cyndi Lauper She Bops
her way out of the 80s
and the printer never runs
out of paper.

Dented Head

Her cat had these peck marks
all over his head
from years of fighting
with captured birds
and when
we got together
he was quite old
and had become
an indoor cat
although he didn't seem
to like that
and now he's long dead,
but I remember his
dented head,
the way my own head feels
when I run my fingers
across it

all the wars
and some of the
peace

a large red line down the middle

the peeling of dry skin
like human wallpaper
that doesn't have
it anymore.

Slow Down

It is the depression all over again.
At least for you.
There are no jobs, keep walking.
Only they call it a slow down now
so as not to induce panic.

Which leads to a slow down
in other ways.

The many arguments.
The kids taken to your mothers
and used as a weapon.

The coffeehouse intellectuals
must always argue their cream.

The man on the street, well, he is just that.
One man on a single street happy with one foot
in front of the other .

And I am that man on the street.
Subject to forces greater than me
and trying to stay afloat.

Knowing
the good times are over
and now it is time for some
of the other.

Hello Brinkmanship!

Can you see me
waving?

Late Fees

Thank god
for the public
library.

We all have
to begin
somewhere.

And I always had late fees
that came out of my weekly allowance
because my father who was cheating on
my mother felt I had to learn
about responsibility.

So I paid the 50 cent fine
each week
and began to believe.

That Isaac Asimov was coming
back from space
and Jules Verne really lived
under the sea.

Stalker Poem

Remember that poem
where Jim Carroll follows
Frank O'Hara around the streets
of New York?

That is the best of the stalker poems.
The best that I have read anyways.

Though I doubt ole Frankie would be much
of a fan.

If someone goes to all the trouble
of following you it may as well
be the feds.

Or some young blonde
with something
busty.

Tremors

in both my hands
while I leave the car
for sideways rain
shaky as the failing
carriage
of a man twice
my age
with this slashing unspoken
horror in my gut
that can never be
digested
knowing the novelty
party shop
full of balloons
has just opened
for business
and that mine
has already
popped.

Her phone
(for Tracey Sivek)

welcomed
her to Canada
even though
she was not in Canada,
close enough
to see snow in May
and speak with an accent,
but the tech
giants were failing
or maybe
they just wanted her
to think
they didn't know
exactly where she was
so they welcomed
her to Canada,
either way,
she had a good laugh
and posted
about it so others
could have
a good laugh too,
even the ones
in Canada
when she was
not.

Black Stretched Limo

We are in the back
of a black stretched limo
for the first time

heading to her mother's house
in Muskoka
from Casino Rama
at cost
because she wants to make
an impression

after the Go Bus up from the city
and the guy who kept smelling his own
armpits for luck

but no one is home
so we walk down to the water
standing over tadpoles
that want to be frogs

enjoying the last of the day
in front of us.

Just Wine

it is just wine
but it looks like blood
on the walls

that frenzied dropping
splatter

now brown
and oxidized
and dried into
the surroundings,

but I promise it is just wine,
I pour fast and write fast
and the walls seem to wear it

the wife gets angry
and I tell her we can just
paint over it when
I'm finished

but I'm never finished

so my pouring station looks
like quite the murder
scene

these days,

like the slaughterhouse
has branched out
into publishing.

Robocalls

It seems like there should be a prize
but there isn't

you hope for some grand gesture at the end
but they just keep moving the finish line
on you

a dirty little trick for sure,
but you are under no obligation
to keep going

even if it seems like there could
be a prize

mercy
in the crackerjack

a tiny felt sticker
of an elephant

and you keep going
we keep going

feeling the light upon our face
and the salt across
our skins

some swill merchant
doing back flips
in your morning breakfast
cereal

robocalls
from the hive
mind

and still no
prize.

Yellow Placemat

There is a war
that no man has ever fought
and died in

no woman
sat over a yellow placemat
and wrote of distant love
into the nether
regions

not for victory
or freedom
or honour

no casket flown home
no flag unfurled

this is my war
and no one
else's.

Invaders Must Die

I never find it advantageous
to get too high.

To disassemble all the electronics
in the house
in a four day sleepless meth binge
while the prodigy assures me
that *Invaders Must Die*.

I have always been suspicious
of Cape Canaveral.

All those rockets into space seem
so much more like Freud
than they do
NASA.

I am much more the sloth
of the endeavour.

If I ever get there at all,
it will be late
and unannounced.

Call me lazy
and you may be
right.

Tag

is that a nip in your pocket
or a mouse?

the new superintendent
is intending

to know see smell hear feel
half the snow globes into
eternal summer

I wish I could tell you there was news,
but you turn on the television
sure as I do

watch Broadway played out
for Bollywood and vice
versa

the way hair and makeup
is brought in to
justify war

I no longer have an address

the name my parents gave to me
has stayed like a boat
of barnacles

if you wish to write, please employ
a competent graffiti artist

I promise to try make out
your name.

When You've Watched Too Many Game Shows

She said her favourite aunt had just died
and I asked her if it was tuberculosis
and she asked for a hug
and I asked her if it was septicemia

and she yelled at me that it was not some quiz show
and then she came in for a hug again

pulling away when I asked her if it was Aids

so that I was pretty sure
it was Aids

for the
win.

Between Handlers

Take the elevator down.
There is something waiting in the lobby
for you that is not an
assassin's bullet.

The cameras of Alfred Stieglitz,
thrice removed.

And it is good that you can checkout
from your room now.

Between handlers
like some rampaging circus elephant
of diminishing trust.

That is the way I feel these days
which means that is the
way I am.

Expecting bullet proof glass
and getting a bouquet
of flowers.

Death lilies
fresh from the slowing
turkey shoot.

And she says she is taking a shower
so I lay on the bed
throw my arms out over
the sides.

Stare up
at a light that will
try to stand in for heaven
for a couple hours.

Imagine

my surprise
when the pigeons
at my feet
squabble over
a single torn shoelace
with no nutritional value
and the guy
who shoulders me
and walks right through
the metal detector
of my back
throws up his arms
absently
and keeps going
as if to say he is sorry
when he is not

his head
full of hair
and his
hair full of product
and him full
of himself
which includes both
his head
and his hair

that is progress
marching on

so that the pigeon
with screaming red
death for eyes
can perch atop
an expired parking
meter

and ogle
the office tower
lunch crowd
through the revolving
door
of the Toronto-Dominion
Centre

downtown.

God was an Irishman with a Fifty Foot Dick

You know that point when you stop yourself
urinating midstream to look in the glass,
that is the god complex right there, some flimsy insufficient
form of control, limited in both scope and distance,
much more of a trickle as you age, I hear the old timers
talk about it like a wife that died 10 years previous, fondly
but still happy she is not there and that makes me sad:
I am hardly a romantic, I am a man of continuance;
I will still be around after the last cockroach has kicked it,
not out of any love of life, but because there should be life
and fuck you.

That is the Irish coming out there. The suicide case
plans to live forever now because you said he couldn't.
Why the English never left that little island of maniacs
alone on their way to empire is beyond me. They could
have saved themselves a world of headaches.

I will be here forever. Even after I am gone.
This is not immorality, just persistence.

Whoa Nellie!

remember when people said
that to one another
as though they were in charge
of livestock?

Female horses in particular.
Seems a little funny now
that you would say that to
another human being,
but it happened.

As if to say:
hold your horses,
even though none of us
had any horses to
hold.

I have a rich cousin who
owns horses now,
but I have never once
uttered the words:
whoa Nellie!
to her.

We haven't spoken in well over 20 years
and maybe that is just as well.

She might tell me: *cowabunga, dude!*
And I wouldn't know what to do
with that.

Live Bait

jump jiminy cricket
the worms of the earth
on the move again

piercing invisible armours
chuckling the bark off trees
paving the roads
with slime

banners in shops
with a bell over the door
that tiny sound of arrival

and the sign in the window
that promises: **Live Bait**

the worms no longer of this earth

and pants that sag below
the middle.

Honest Assessment

I think I have gone insane.
There is no evidence to the contrary.
All I have are these words,
my work.

It is up to you
to decide.

Thread Count

Sit alone
on your bed
with a comfortable
thread count

10 000 miles from home

knowing the flowers in the hall
just outside your door
are replaced each day
like sentry duty

and the chlorine in the pool
will kill any urine
and half your sperm count
in a single sitting

and the man at the bar
is amicable Yakuza

the reason he is missing no fingers
is that he is good at his job

that is what you have decided
swatting imaginary spiders
off your shoulders
in plausible increments

knowing your room is closer
than a fifteen hour flight
back to hell

and that it only takes
a single murderous silver elevator
to get back there

past the flowers that never die

into a room someone who believes in you
has paid for.

Leg Work

There
is
nowhere
else

to
turn.

All
the
lefts
and
rights

have
been

taken.

This is Where They Killed the President

We land at Dallas/Ft. Worth
after a long flight
and we all get up at the same time
and are stuck.

And this old timer keeps pushing
deep into my back.

It is a connector
and my medications
have long run out.

Then he pushes my wife back into
other passengers.

Stop!, she yells,
you are hurting me.

She could see the look in my eyes.
It was the closest I have ever come
to killing a man.

She leaned into me with the bags
so I could not turn around.

I threw my ass out
to knock the bastard
across the seats.

Just hoping he would say something.
Last words are always important.

THIS IS WHERE THEY KILLED THE PRESIDENT!,
I growled.

So much for the friendly skies.

And after a full night's sleep
and pills I am glad I did not end up
in a Texas prison.

We travel smarter now.
No connectors, plenty of pills.

Letting all the others get off first
even when we are in a hurry.

Making up time some other way.
We are most efficient
when we have
to be.

Wantling

Man, they were rough on Hemingway
and the meats.

Always after their death, of course.
The living never fear the dead.

Not in this lifetime.
Where stainless steel appliances
have replaced actual
hauntings.

And smacked Willie Wantling never left Korea
so they could never hold him
in the many lost hours of San Quentin.

All those years for forgery and possession
never enough to slime a snail
back out of its
shell.

Back into Korea,
the Asian mainland.

Back into the heart
of the mind
that never leaves
you.

The One

I'd hate to be the one
who actually gets it,
I confess to her,
after a lifetime of abuse
and neglect
horror
and humiliation

I imagine they'd be dead
with the first couple
blows

nothing held back
all that honest
pain

pure butchery

and they give you a release
that you finally
take.

Protests

We walk by the latest protests
down by the parliament
hand in hand

as many ski mask men
lob Molotov cocktails
into the police line
full of shields

hoping for a royal flush
out of two pair

and back at her place
she lights a smoke
and flips through the pages
of a Penthouse Magazine
telling me all the girls I like
are frigid

so that
I will sleep
with her
and none of
the others

which remain
fresh in my mind

and always in
play.

Business (2)

cut rate
in my wandering
eye

and I never mix business
and pleasure

because pleasure becomes
business

which has a domineering streak

leeching into everything
sucking out all the enjoyment
until you can't remember
the last time

there was anything
but business.

White Feather

snow peas are expensive out of season
and I think of tiny Picasso
handed a white feather in the streets
of Paris
by the many haughty women
during the war
as though he were a coward
when he wasn't even
French

and I can just imagine
those smoldering molten
eyes

boiling over

knowing idiocy
has just bested him

and the way he must have run
back to his studio
to capture it all,
in love with the giant
Andalusian brush
of himself.

Factory Direct

Some crazy shot Warhol
so we had to open our own
soup cans.

And I give him credit.
He always knew the hospital
would kill him
and it did.

Intuition is a powerful monkey.
Even if you're from Pittsburgh.

I guess that Blow Job movie
made them really mad.

But that is the chance you take
with your art.

Everyone's a critic.
And some of them
are armed.

Yule Log

Three of us
in that drunken
new year's hallway
long as espionage

arguing over the meaning
of a Yule log
because I had just returned
from the bathroom
and found a large winding
offering sitting down in
the bowl

and complimenting him on the stinking brown
ability of his colon,
I tell him I found his yule log

to which he asks me if I even know
what a yule log is

which I don't,
but is sounds long
and purposeful

so that I know I must be right
even in this state

as his drunken girlfriend
falls into the wall
and laughs
at our ridiculous clown show
offering

shouting:
YOU GUYS ARE IDIOTS!

so that I know just how she sounds
during sex.

Ask My Dust

It is horrible to think that you have failed.
Fante should be read like the Gideons
in hotel side tables before extramarital sex.

Who made the bible Shakespeare?
Necessary reading like the liner notes
to Iron Maiden's *The Number of The Beast*?

Fante's L.A. is riddled with catholic guilt.
Like a sandbox that knows it is dirty.

And apprehension is important.
It adds traffic to the streets.

You should already know this.
Which means I have failed.

Nursing Presentation

She has been awake all night.
Working on her nursing presentation
for the bridging program through Nipissing.

And when I come down in the morning
it is there.

A large Bristol board offering
at the bottom of the stairs
that looks better than I ever have
on a good day.

As though Capricorn Santa
has been by to fill all the ice trays
and take out the garbage.

And when she wakes up,
she needs to hear it.

That she has done good.
That is our weakness.
We work on a reward system.

I tell her there is nothing wrong
with a man or woman taking pride in their work,
that Kevin Spacey in *Seven* said so.

She hugs me
and says that is just what
she needed to hear.

I noogie her head
and pull her in tight
like a stone cold
professional.

This day
will be a good one
because we have decided
it is ours

and no one
else's

and we are just
starting.

Vanticide

Rent a van, it is easy,
drive up over the curb
plowing into pedestrians,
the terror is in the democracy
of the act,
that such things can happen
anywhere like sneezing into
your hand
and making complete
strangers sick for weeks.

If the term ever goes Viral
I deserve royalties.

That is how we put method
to mouth
in the capitalist
era.

Really nail Adam Smith
down to the price
of gold.

Follow a bull
to market
until we all

get the
horns.

To those who call paper parchment

you are achieving nothing by dragging
the past into the present,
porcupines have quills and they
do not write a thing;
you do not write with quills
or I would assume you were writing
with a porcupine
which does not make you sound
refined at all,
just obnoxious and semantically
wrong.

Demolition Expert

Democracy or tyranny,
I think more people are growing
wise to the company brew.

And asking themselves,
what's the difference?

There is none, of course,
but you have to baby step
the legs out of walking.

Undo
all that has been
done.

It won't be pretty
or easy.

And those that don't want to believe
never will.
They are the backbone.

The thing
that must be broken.

And I'm not even
one of the politicos,
just imagine
what they see.

It won't be pretty.
That same single phrase
keeps coming back
to me.

Tectonic

Can you believe that earthquake that
never happened?

I started shakin' all over like Elvis
in protest.

And the aftershocks were more
of a mild palsy.

Past girlfriends checking on their plates
in a psychic sense.

An Answer

a
man

who
gives
you
everything

can
never
mean
nothing

after
that,

that
is
the
heart
I
found
again

after

so

many

years,

by

weeding

through

the

lost

&

found

and

pulling

out

something

that

was

almost

never

mine.

Renege

I was going to write a poem,
but now I don't want to

I want to sit with hours of cold beer
and good music

and do nothing

I want to sit on the couch
wasting the light of the day

toss the coaster at the wall
like a wet ninja star

just stop typing, I tell my fingers,
it's easy.

Uncivil is the War

They beam pictures back
from Syria
and I think to myself:
what did you expect?

War is brutal
and civil wars are
the worst.

And you went and armed
one side
and let someone else
arm the other
and now you are surprised
when the mud
got dirty.

And it is the people that lose.
It is always the people.
While competing interests compete
at interest.

What did you expect?

Always Cry Wolf

Ball of hair in the waste basket,
I have never once wanted
you back.

This is not a simple rebound.
Some pandering cold Farley Mowat novel
tripping over the great wide open.

The sign over the door down at missing persons
so optimistically reading:
Don't Be A Stranger

and I think about the children
on the backs of milk cartons,
the sheer number of cows that have
gone into our general
milking.

If history has anything to teach us,
it is to not be history.

Even the present is just a dog
down at the track
chasing the simple lure
of the future
in circles

so you can bet
on it.

Visible Minority

I'm left handed
so I represent only ten percent
of the world's population
and yet I am not a visible minority.

Even though I hold everything in my left hand.
Which is visible to everybody.

But that is not enough.
I am the wrong kind
of minority.

There are no benefits for me.
No understanding.

Everything is right handed.
Right down to all the doors I open.

Everything is backwards.
And no one cares.

All Those Stairs

I am losing feeling in my right hand.
All those stairs.

Dating sites are recycling plants with pictures.
All those stairs.

See you in port-wine stain space.
All those stairs.

Shaking wands of the Harry Potter franchise.
All those stairs.

I am my own personal filibuster.
All those stairs.

Pick of the litter.
All those stairs.

Triple bypass on quadruple highways.
All those stairs.
All those stairs.

Your presence should be
a celebration.

St. Patrick's Day, 2018

I guess I am drinking,
but I am putting in the heavy lifting
wrestling with the word again
so it's not really the same thing.

Not at all like that army of screaming
drunken green beer idiots
in little green hats
playing Irish for
a day.

I have never celebrated the occasion
because of what it has become.

I have never even been to the parades.
The largest are in Dublin and New York
I am told.

Chicago turned its water green
and it just looks like what I imagine
comes out of the taps most days.

Some festive radioactive green sludge.
The reason your children have thirteen toes
and a tiny head on the back like
a rear view mirror for life.

But you have the most Irish name ever!,
my wife screams.

That is true.
And I am proud of that fact.
But I will still be in bed by ten o'clock
tonight.

Another long day on the hustle.
With work in the morning.

Trying to make good
with so many others on
the make.

Hell, even Joyce only gets the retro love.
Back in the day he was censored and bankrupted
and banished from the island.

Hated for his clean vulgar allegiance
to the truth.

The Irish swallow their own.

I am Canadian,
so I am only Irish
by proxy.

Which means there is a chance for me.

My grandfather left
and now I am coming
back.

But never with all the others.
This life is mine and mine
alone.

The individual mind
and the individual
way.

I want my words to seem space rock rare.
Like loves you lose and always remember.

Something
you can never get back
and spend the rest of your life
trying to.

So imagine my aversion to green beer.
How soundly I will sleep out of
my own misguided drunkenness.

White Devil

The price
is never the
price

when you marry
into the market

a white devil
in one of the
stans

speculating for big oil
and an apartment
that doesn't come
with other
apartments

something
with a view
so the legally blind
can be jealous

in central
Asia.

Dizzy

Do not
speak out
of turn

there
are only
so many roundabouts
and one way to spell
dizzy

if I could wrap my head
around any of this
you could put a bow
on it
and scream:
CHRISTMAS!

Do not
wait for turtles
to come out
of their
shell

the dark
is only dark

because you refuse
to turn on the
lights.

I am not here
to wave fingers
in the wind.

All my heroes
are dead.

Tall Cans

Sitting up in bed
with a couple of tall cans
from the Walgreens across the street

watching a family of fake edited drug smugglers
find themselves in under two hours
on TNT

and the sloppy car wreck way the black leather headboard
looks as though spent sweat lodges are tossing tired
Indian head pennies at it
like a 2 in 1 shampoo you complain about
on the other side of dandruff

and we are away from home
like Erik the Red

for the first time

avoiding the penny slots
like the plague.

A fight

in the schoolyard
is not what it used
to be.

Nothing to the death
and always on
camera.

Many screaming girls breaking it up
after the first punch.

And the ocean
is far away
and your tears are closer
than that.

Headlock hipsters in the street
in the way of honking
traffic.

Staples

The sales kid
in the office furniture section
of the local staples

comes smiling fresh off his lunch
and says I fell into that chair
as if it was meant
for me

and I know he is working on commission
and meant nothing by it

that the popped whiteheads on his face
know nothing of Krakatoa,

but I immediately stand up
and walk away as though
I have just left the
plague

out into a parking lot
with many parked cars
in it.

28th

The 28th poem of the night
is hardly something to write home
about.

You have greased the wheels
and passed through that sweet spot
and entered that regretful sloppy
slurring phase that proves that Hunter Thompson
rode the broken horse of artistic licence
right out of town.

Try it if you don't believe me.
Imbibe yourself as they say.

Throw your legs up behind your ears
and scream
in the good name of flexibility.

Product Placement

If I was so sure of myself
there would be a lot
less words.

Language is not meant to communicate
so much as it betrays.

Just follow that silver tongue
all the way back to morning after
regret.

Do not blame the gecko,
too much to drink is not a lizard
thing.

You indulged and got tipsy
and fell for the used car
salesman.

Take it on the chin
and move on.

No one likes a
sore loser.

Just look at all the rejects
in conference room D.

Championing the sanctity
of product placement
in suits that make them
look like monuments

instead of real
people.

Drain Cover

We have taken the money
back from taxes
and gone through a full bathroom reno
right down to the studs
to fix a leak that was coming through
the kitchen ceiling whenever
we showered

and after a week of work
we have our brand new shower
with all the fixings

but it is missing the drain cover

so the wife has taken to writing the company
which has promised to send one along

which is merely decorative, of course,
a small thing to some,
but even the tax money won't
cover the cost

bathrooms are expensive

so we want it done
right

with one of those new fangled
shower heads that look more like
a stainless steel cricket paddle
and have so many buttons that
I am still learning how not to burn
myself.

Venture Capital

The capital of Venture was Telescopeopolis
and many of its citizens were of a seafaring bent,
others looked to the sky like so many do to yoga instructors
today, facing down their dogs
and when chances were taken, everyone took them
inviting the gains and accepting the losses
and when animals were sacrificed I would venture
that they would have preferred another
vocation, perhaps grazing somewhere outside the city walls
which were manned by archers that never once
thought of Cupid.

Breaking Silence, Breaking Wind

The glass falls to the floor,
I cannot stop breaking things.
Just last week it was my silence
and now I am breaking wind.

I know of many broken homes,
but I have nothing to do with that.

Those broken pistachios, my handiwork,
so is that broken ice that makes conversation
such a cinch.

I used to break horses for the movie people
and bad habits for the habit police.
Eggs, well yes, who hasn't?

Piñatas, hearts, bread, news stories, windows,
glow sticks, world records…

Some people will pay you to break legs.
Hardly ever their own, but there is a market
for that as well.

The New Minimalism

let's just say
I am not the father of
the New Minimalism
right off

never coined the phrase
and everything

didn't trademarked the shit
out of that thing
like simplicity
at a corporate level

so that money could be made
from the written word

in a world that wants everything
to be difficult

where people cross the street
to get to the other
side.

Bark

I have an allergy.
I am allergic to people.
No one respects my allergy.
They are people.

That is how an allergy works.
Respect it, until you are it.
Then the gloves are off.
Really dig into the background.

Build a new devil
so the rest can know
of god.

Which leaves me hanging.
Glory is a hot sauce with all the
fine trimmings.

People line up for blocks
for the bark.

Even the tree of knowledge
wasn't this popular.

Seems all you need these days
is a smoker and thirteen hours
and word of mouth.

No better barbecue
this side of San Antone.

Right along the side
of the road
like a flat.

Sewer Cake

The boys
that never came home
from of the war
are bad enough,
but I am one of the boys
that never had
a home,
my war has no beginning
or end;
the reason was never there
and the horror goes on
and on...

$3 Dollar Movies

were the
best

and we went to them
many times
a week

when we were dating

at Yonge and
Dundas

catching the underground
back out of the city

when we were done
with it

and ready to start in
on the lips

of each
other.

Penny Slots

oh, hallelujah
god bless

the penny slots
are spitting out the devil's
poison again

under lights
from the super church
pulpit

a serpent of riches
breaking bank

this is Babel
3 for 1 Gomorrah

praise the almighty
the Nazarene

big winner
on the floor

pit boss escort
back to the betting
windows,

amen.

Shoot Me Before I Shoot You

Shoot me before I shoot you. Of course, I do not have a gun. Not even one of those cheap water guns that come in birthday party kiddie bags and fail after three squeezes. The blue ones always looked the coolest, though they never worked any better than the rest. But there is something to be said for appearance. Why else would we spend more on it than education? Hell, appearance is a trillion dollar industry. If we can't be what we want, we may as well look the part. And that's where hair and make-up comes in. And wardrobe. And an army of *product* with marketable feel good names. Who doesn't want to be beautiful? Have you seen those gargoyles hanging off the sides of buildings? They look ugly as sin. Someone should shoot them all. Put them out of their misery. Preferably with a military grade assault rifle because everything is bigger in Texas. You don't want to just shoot the damn thing, you want to send its vital organs back to the dark ages. See, time travel is a real thing. Like the Yeti. And sitting up in bed I get to thinking how the camera lobby is trying to shoulder in on all our guns. Cameras should be banned from shooting anyone that guns can shoot. It is a question of morality. God made guns and the devil made the camera. What side are you on? We have to protect our protection. The South Beach Diet demands it.

A Man in Lifts
Wants to be Carted Around
like a False Ladder

Seat yourself
in the penthouse
of the tallest building
in Australasia

and you are still 5 ft.5

with a father that never
stuck around

and standing under a morning
showerhead that may as well
be Everest

the way room service
always looks surprised
at the door

knowing it has lost its tip
because it knows what
you know,

that a man in lifts
wants to be carted around
like a false ladder

while the jobsite of his marriage
falls apart at home.

Quick Strike

The best poems
read like a bombing.

Simple, direct
and by surprise.

A quick strike
and then you are out.

The Ramones
playing 16 songs in 14 minutes
because people are busy
and have lives
to live.

So you do your thing
and then you are
gone.

Just like that.

A Death in the Family

Someone is fighting a battle and losing
and someone else is up in the attic
looking through old boxes after a death
in the family

that army of dust that invades everything
black mold over all the insulation

and someone is picking up a cake
and someone else is helping a friend
move a couch

and I am squashing a bug
and Atlantis is nowhere to be found

and you are reading this poem

which should probably end
right now.

After Lively

We round
that familiar Sudbury
turnoff

after Lively

and I think of how the local Walmart
wants you to drive past the bubbling cesspool
and backup

to prices you can
afford

and how she signed me
out of the madhouse
so we could have lunch together
four years ago

against those parking space barricades
talking the voice out of
influenza

and how the world seems so insane
now even without me
in it.

Smash Up

Two groups of football fans
from opposing teams
agree to meet at a specific time
and place in uniform
to have it out

and there is a very clannish feeling
to it all

banging their chests
in competing song
for the land

and the single paralysing scream
as the first wave of each
slam into each other

how the ones in black
dominate the ones in red
that retreat and leave
a few of their fallen
behind

to be kicked in the head
a couple more times

as they curl up in the dirt
and wait for the end
of it to come

as it always
does.

Daisy Dukes

Your mother
leaves home for
work.

Your father left home
for prison ten years
ago.

And your older brother
was shot dead in a shooting
because of a shooting because
of a shooting…

You looked up to him
the same way skyscrapers
dominate the afternoon sky,
but you would never
admit it.

You are tough now.
Like rubbery chicken.

No one can tell you
what to do
except for your boss

and your mother
and the law
and traffic signals

and everyone
else…

I bet you fashion yourself
a real gangster.

Talk up girls
in their daisy dukes.

Repeating the pattern.

Without ever learning
how to use the
anger.

To channel all that frustration
into a whole new way

of
exploding.

It is silly

how many poems
I have lost to drunkenness

all these nights
closing poems instead
of saving them

not even realizing
what I have
done

and when you print out
and come back to the books
you realize a large part
of what you said
is no longer
there.

you try to forget it,
but such things are a part
of you

still,
you don't let it eat you up,
this is not simple
cannibalism

the same way the power cuts
out when you're in a groove

and you wake up the next morning
to reset the clock
and begin
again.

Crash Dummy

The market will crash
sure as cars
crash.

I am not an expert
or pundit
or anything
else.

Just a simple pair of eyes
with no dog in
this fight.

Knowing the house of parliament
will always fail inspection.

Blow the nose

and things are
open

what came before is the past

it is complicated
like inviting lunch over to dinner
and trying to explain
this latest betrayal

that every ancient civilization
is nothing more than a pyramid scheme
that wants you to invest:

in the wheel
and the fire
and the firewall
and cryogenics

some time by the pool
is always good

Conference room B
full of conferences that
never lead to
anything
and my sinuses are cleared now

like all the gangly flops
of Dick Fosbury
before the White Sox
threw the 1919
World Series

and we pretended
to know anything
about sex

as though the orgasm
was just a dinosaur
brought back
to screaming
life.

Sloppy Glow Stick EDM

She wants me to hit her G-spot.
This requires a marksman.
Someone cool through the scope.
Army background.
A loner.
Controlled breathing.

I am a mess.
Elton John seems more like a planet
than a simple man to me.

Chewing down anti-depressants
to sloppy glow stick EDM.

Flicking snails
off the back screen door
so they can imagine wormholes
without the shell.

Compact Car Rentals

To spend your whole life
in a spin cycle.

I am thinking of my parents now.

That busy long hours way
they avoided each other
in spite of all those happy
Burton Avenue wedding
pictures.

Divorce is a good thing.

Not for the children,
but the lawyers clean up
nicely.

I am thinking of compact car rentals now.

How sewing machines can be driven
through the streets of Los Angeles
for $30 a day.

And the long flight back to civilization.

To syphoned gas
and morning coffee.

And a job to do that is never done.

And a boss
that is never
happy.

Basketball Net

Cortisone shots
for the pain

a human addiction
before they know
why footnotes are so
important

family headstones
and dinner table racism

fires burn
because of human
accelerants

all those shortcomings
personified

the old failing the young
and the young failing
themselves

brand name shoes
no longer
enough

and standing under this
basketball net
I understand Samoa
as a hug

and passivity as an ocean

Quixote's windmills
waving bye to
reason

the Dutch
flooding tulips
in times of orange
war

and all this medical
marijuana I pass on the street
like a zombie apocalypse
of the living

standing in lines long as
expired coupon
eternity

waiting on credit card
debt to clear

so the modern world
can be modern

and all the rest of us
can try to look
retro

in the death fangs
of the spider

that lives beside
your bed.

Yo-Yo Man

A failing sun of twine
from yo-yo man fingers
and you marvel the way you did
the first time your father took you
to the circus to watch the acrobats
and cheer for death;
the way he said removing the net
below was like going to bed
with your mother
and the elephant who stood
on a ball, you could see yourself
in that cowering grey giant,
the man with the whip always
behind you: father, teacher,
your first night on the job;
any job you can still remember
like pulling knife fights out
of a bloody hat
and yo-yo man is here
for your money,
going town-to-town
pulling his kite of a sun
behind him
so your dreams can make
money for someone
else.

Flying Pig…Revisited

The best way to release an album
is to reimagine it a giant inflatable chicken
that sails over the city
giving people who have nothing to
talk about curious slimy mouths,
fingers pointing through the air like
wrinkled obelisks,
that flying pig…revisited;
the one that shut down Heathrow
only now it is a chicken which makes one
think of the Blitz, large German eggs dropped
from the heavens, but this is just an album
by a band; a sorry stunt for radio play.

Someone should give the sky a comb over.
The clouds look ridiculous when they part
in the middle.

Good Tidings and All that Stuff

I am coming to the end of things,
winding down.
I can feel it.
What came before was lacking
both in scope and sincerity
and what comes next is anyone's
guess.

The body, heart and mind
all breaking down.

I have felt it for some time.
A 300 year old man in a 39 year old
body.

Still,
for a depressed cynic heroin child
of the 90s
I am oddly optimistic.

Something always comes.

It may not be what you want.
But it will always be what
you need.

As long as the young
are never the old
and always

the
young.

There is nothing
without the
spirit.

To push things along.

Those that take chances
in spite of their mortal
selves.

Protagonist Zero

rational is he who coifs all the hair in the wig shop
rational is he who opens a tattoo parlour of kindness that refuses
    to scar anyone
rational is he who drinks under tables so no one can ever drink
    him under the table first
rational is he biting into many restroom urine pucks of yellow
    contrition
rational is he who forms his own line in the shower and waits
    on soap
rational is he that eats nothing but donkey shavings for 26 days
rational is he shovelling all the snow out of Siberia
rational is he who used to be a she according to the literature
rational is he that jars his own preserves and cans his own ass
rational is he when he screams *FAKE NEWS!* each time the
    elderly take out their teeth before bed
rational is he who castrates himself at the ballpark during
    the 7th inning stretch
rational is he who accuses elevators of being heaven on the cheap
rational is he in man bun coffee shops soaking up the hyperbole
    as though he were a fair trade dishrag of popular
    condemnation
rational is he on horseback riding his broomstick around
    the apartment
rational is he who holds down a job like a submarine under
    water

rational is he paying state tax in national parks
rational is he starting a cab service full of the first
    passengerless cars
rational is he who worships the drink fountain as liquid amnesia
rational is he who names all his kids after hurricanes,
    then buysbeachfront property and waits
rational is he in bright yellow pajamas that may as well be
    the sun
rational is he taking apart all the light fixtures after four pots
    of coffee
rational is he who runs into a burning building to preserve
    the honour of water
rational is he who lives at the library because that is where
    they keep all the books
rational is he walking everywhere in someone else's shoes
rational is he growing a beard to fight deforestation and only
    dating girls with names that start with O
rational is he who lets his hair stand on end so he can be taller
rational is he who keeps Basho beside his bed, and at least
    three cats in it at all times
rational is he collecting dust instead of stamps
rational is he who throws consecutive games of checkers and
    thinks in terms of trajectory
rational is he who moves his bowels before he ever considers
    moving anywhere himself
rational is he that wears layers because you can never be hidden
    enough
rational is he considering a bag of rotten pears just spoilt ballots
    by other means

rational is he sitting at the ballet waiting for Judas Priest
    to come on
rational is he making love seats into the new Haight-Ashbury
rational is he who organizes his crime into *occasions*
rational is he who runs for president of a bike club, then
    shows up on a unicycle
rational is he putting in flower planters so the cyborgs
    will have something nice to look at when they take over
rational is he waiting for planes to be grounded and grievances
    to be aired
rational is he paying bills in tight jeans in the dark on a
    Wednesday with all the children of woe
rational is he buzzing strangers into his building so that
    murder can happen
rational is he who trusts no one that can't whistle
rational is he deboning fish on a ratty boat launch in the sticks
rational is he who thinks of the Napoleonic Wars as extra
    toppings
rational is he who holds up the flag of every known country,
    casting as wide a net as possible on love
rational is he who stands in strange driveways believing
    himself the family hatchback
rational is he fighting goldfish because cockfights are cruel
    and popular and profitable
rational is he who believes the electrical box out front is
    always humming something by the Temptations
rational is he who looks for furry shanks among the prison
    population at the zoo

rational is he sitting in fast food restaurants
    with something in the slow cooker
rational is he slamming doors in the face of windows
rational is he climbing into a storage box and waiting for
    someone to move him
rational is he starting at the end of a novel and working
    his way back to protagonist zero
rational is he who writes with a pen, but dreams in pencil
rational is he…rational is she
rational   rational   rationale
rational is he on the outskirts
of town,
of fashion.

Face Fronds

(Buffy Sainte-Marie never cussed out
a newly waxed floor)

I kept my secret

(daddy's ragamuffin
in the melon core)

I kept my secret

(kinda right in a roundabout way)

I kept my secret
I kept my secret

(face fronds for eyebrows with bushiness
lost to palms)

I kept my secret
from everyone.

PTSD # 112

I find myself running
even though I don't
know why
there is a fear that has me
both paralysed and running
at the same time
and the sound of helicopters
overhead but I can't
look up out of dread
and I keep running barefoot
feeling the gravel stones
against my feet
the wandering lights
of alien abduction or
something worse
and I am breathing through
a blue balaclava with effort
I can feel the wet of the spittle
back against my face
and running inside one of my
childhood high schools
I take refuge in the stairwell
with this kid who smiles
and can't grow a moustache
that sticks a knife in me
once he is close enough
and spits something warm
over my body as I die.

Grayson

jacked a truck
out of Brandon
on its way to Winnipeg
and made
the driver get out
and walk
during the unforgiving
mosquito season
which is a cruel thing
to do in these parts
and by the time
the man was picked up
he had been
eaten alive,
looked like one of those
Ellis Islanders
under quarantine,
and Grayson barely made
it off the reserve
before johnny law closed
the highway
and tacked the road
so that
when the truck
blew its tires

it rolled down into
a ditch
with ole' Grayson
and 17 skids
of raw tobacco
along with
it.

One of Micheline's
(for Brenton Booth)

this
no bullshit wordsmith
from down under
started this
no bullshit magazine
called The Asylum Floor
and he
got in touch with
Jack Micheline's son
who said
he could look
through his father's paintings
and choose one
for the cover of the second
issue which may not
be a big deal
in the circles you travel,
but you can bet
your ass
it's like Mardi Gras
in these
parts.

Gloomy Dean

They found a dead body
two streets away from here
with the winter thaw:

ubi saeva indignatio ulterius
cor lacerare nequit

That is how such things go
in the great white north.

It takes a while to find anyone.
Everything is underserviced.

And I think I know who the murderer is.
There was an incident about eight months ago
where some idiot followed a girl
into the women's bathroom
at the public pool
and tried to make out
with her.

Her boyfriend intervened
and beat the crap out of the guy
who took his lumps and
ran off.
The boyfriend is the dead body.
I think I know who did the deed.

I could be totally wrong.
Keep in mind this is supposed
to be a piece of fiction.

Like Gulliver's Travels.

Swift has never been one of my favourites,
but I have a few of his books.

Tell me his Houyhnhnmys
were not pinched by Orwell
for his farm.

Hell,
even Kubrick took his flying island
for Strangelove.

That is what artists do.
They take.

And murderers too.

Which is how I got started
on this whole clumsy
yarn.

My savage
indignation.

Full Circle

not just a half circle,
that would be
lazy

like picking up a Frisbee
and refusing to
throw it

or watching a partial eclipse
make a complete fool
of itself –

CIRCUMFRENCE!
I hear the entire math department
yell

which sounds like a sex toy to me
or an old pagan ritual involving many
many sheets of particle board and a bag
of coloured marshmallows

ALL THE WAY AROUND!
I hear the cinder track coach
beckon

a stopwatch in his hand
and a lucky marble in his pocket
which he strokes three times
when he thinks no one
is looking.

Hallway

The hallway is taller than a whole team of basketball players
lying down, what a strange notion to have,
this long darkened hallway between apartments
of chipped linoleum and bloody bandages,
the screaming red numbers of the alarm clock:
 2:37…8…9…2:40
the experts say it is morning, but it is very dark out
you have to feel your way around like pin the tail on the donkey
all over again only you are on your own this time
and the fridge is full of food and the landlord is full of himself
and the shoes by the door never walk off with each other;
you admire their loyalty to the cause, the boa constrictor
of their laces that could strangle a man but instead show
deference –
my shoes are saints for the unofficial canon,
we walk everywhere together…
even down this long sleepless hallway
with smoky crawling walls of nicotine darkness.

No Question of Ownership

turn away from the beast
your guts are still your guts
even when they spill
out of you

there is no question of ownership
though you should probably keep
the papers

those careful words
you can no longer sit for
in a frenzy

and it is advantageous
to think of freeway on ramps
as stitches that hold it
all together

while you claw and thirst
and gnarl
and chew

in that fury
that has always
been with
you.

Ryan Quinn Flanagan is a Canadian-born author who lives in Elliot Lake, Ontario, Canada with his wife and many bears that rifle through his garbage. His work has been published both in print and online in such places as: *The New York Quarterly, Evergreen Review, Cultural Weekly, The Rye Whiskey Review* and *The Oklahoma Review*. He enjoys listening to the blues and cruising down the TransCanada is his big blacked out truck.

www.ingramcontent.com/pod-product-compliance
Lightning Source LLC
Chambersburg PA
CBHW030106100526
44591CB00009B/302